Praise for *The VESPA Handbook*

Martin Griffin and Steve Oakes clearly understand what makes both students and their teachers tick! In this highly practical handbook, they've taken leading-edge educational research and combined it with their own teaching experience to create a host of easy-to-follow activities, many of which can be completed in the brief window of tutorial time. This is a fantastically rich resource that should be required reading for anyone working with young people who aren't yet fulfilling their potential – it should certainly be on the bookshelf of every head of sixth form.

Becky Cox, School Effectiveness Adviser, HFL Education

There's a lot to love in *The VESPA Handbook*. I really like the fact that it's rooted in reality and is extremely useful for the teacher who has concerns for all their students. The advice and direction offered to teachers is exemplary, privileging honest attainment and success at a human level, which, in turn, makes the handbook indispensable. I'm grateful to Martin and Steve for writing it.

Hywel Roberts, teacher and writer

This book superbly builds upon the first editions by enabling students and teachers to deliver activities bespoke to need. Activities you can pick up and deliver that need no previous study or experience can be used by schools and colleges to support their learners in a variety of capacities to enable both academic and well-being progress. With a keen focus on developing metacognitive skills and enabling learners to self-evaluate their own development needs, it encourages educational practitioners to think beyond the curriculum and more about key life skills essential for learners' ongoing transitional journey to further and higher levels of study and career pathways. These activities will definitely refresh and uplift the VESPA model further.

Siân Farquharson, Post-16 Professional Learning Lead Partner, Education Achievement Service

Post-pandemic, nothing is quite what it once was. More students than ever seem to need extra support to enable them to study effectively. This latest book in the brilliant VESPA series acknowledges things have changed. This handbook provides teachers with a superbly curated set of new activities for students, which are organised upon the original VESPA structure but are shaped to address the new normal in the classroom. It's an essential resource for anyone trying to boost students' commitment to their studies.

John Tomsett, erstwhile head teacher, consultant and author

Steve and Martin have the incredible ability to frame ideas and suggestions to develop learner habits in a way which just simply makes sense to teachers and students alike. Their research is relevant, and their suggestions are presented in an inviting style while challenging our students to truly reflect on how they are as learners and how they could be much more successful. A true staple of a successful curriculum.

Suzanne Ingram, Deputy Head Teacher, Spalding Grammar School

The VESPA Handbook begins with a vital question: what are the characteristics and behaviours of successful students? In this fascinating student guide, Oakes and Griffin explore the mindsets and practices of successful students, using their findings to help readers achieve similarly impressive results. With a range of sensible strategies and a wealth of practical advice, this is the perfect book for students who are keen to improve their study skills and reach their full academic potential.

Mark Roberts, English teacher and Director of Research, Carrickfergus Grammar School

The VESPA Handbook

VISION – EFFORT – SYSTEMS – PRACTICE – ATTITUDE

40 new activities to boost student commitment, motivation and productivity

Steve Oakes and Martin Griffin

Crown House Publishing Limited
www.crownhouse.co.uk

First published by
Crown House Publishing
Crown Buildings,
Bancyfelin,
Carmarthen,
Wales, SA33 5ND, UK
www.crownhouse.co.uk

and

Crown House Publishing Company LLC
PO Box 2223, Williston, VT 05495, USA
www.crownhousepublishing.com

First published 2024.

British Library Cataloguing-in-Publication Data

A catalogue entry for this book is available from the British Library.

Print ISBN: 978-178583710-4
Mobi ISBN: 978-178583719-7
ePub ISBN: 978-178583720-3
ePDF ISBN: 978-178583721-0
LCCN: 2024932494

Printed and bound in the UK by
TJ Books, Padstow, Cornwall

Authors' Note

Imagine you're set this challenge.

Every day, you must arrive at a designated room at a specific time. Once there, you're given a jigsaw piece. The piece will be small, the image on it an elusive and unreadable splinter of something bigger.

The next day, you're going to show up and be given a second piece. It will fit into the first. There's still not enough to speculate about what image might be represented, but the following day you'll get a third, and it will fit the first two.

You're going to keep collecting pieces a day at a time for two years. Sometimes the new bits you receive will fit with pieces you already have, but sometimes – and this comes as a surprise – they'll seem to be entirely unrelated. Sometimes you'll be given duplicates of pieces you've already collected – this will feel frustrating. And sometimes you'll get pieces that seem to belong to different jigsaws altogether.

Sometimes the images on the pieces are sharp and recognisable, and at other times they'll be fuzzy. Since you're only human, on occasion you'll lose pieces you've been given in the past. Now and again, you'll forget to slip the day's piece into its slot when you get home and wind up a week later with a jumbled pile of homeless pieces.

There are days when you'll be unwell and miss a delivery, and if this happens often enough, gaps will open up in your jigsaw, weakening the overall picture. To make matters worse, when you look back at older pieces, you'll find that whatever image was once there has begun to mysteriously fade.

When your two years are up, you'll have pieces running into many hundreds. Your final challenge will be to assemble this multitude of components and then demonstrate your complete understanding of the picture shown. And you'll take a test, the results of which will have the potential to change the course of your life.

Oh, and you're building maybe ten jigsaws simultaneously. Good luck!

Let's stay with this metaphor just a little while longer. What skills might you need to complete this epic task successfully?

When you're learning something in increments like this, two years is a long time. There are going to be days – whole weeks even – when you'll wonder why you're bothering, so you're going to need to figure out how to stay motivated, imagining a positive outcome down the line. And, since that jigsaw doesn't build itself, you'll need the determination to get out of bed every day, collect your piece and think hard about where it fits with the others.

Other skills spring to mind: storing your pieces will be crucial – losing them, misplacing them or leaving them scattered randomly will destroy your ability to read the image. There's also the issue of the fading pieces to tackle; without proper attention, those colours will bleach to nothingness. And what of the psychological pressures? That test at the end looks scary; you'll need to develop the ability to handle stress, beat frustration and remain optimistic, even during setbacks.

Where some education books focus on how individual teachers might sequence and deliver pieces of information in the clearest, most helpful and supportive way, engaging as many learners as possible, this one is different.

It looks at how we might help learners to manage the process of acquiring each new jigsaw piece of knowledge and skill. We're going to be exploring the characteristics, qualities and habits of successful students, and we'll share forty replicable tools and tactics that all students can use immediately in and out of the classroom – activities that will help them to set goals, work more efficiently, organise their resources, revise more effectively and solve problems.

All of which is going to help them build better jigsaws.

email: info@vespa.academy

X: @VESPAmindset

Acknowledgements

Many thanks to the wonderful team at Crown House for their patience and positivity during the writing of this book. A lot has changed since we first put pen to paper five years ago – not least the concept, the title, the scope and much of the content. And that's without mentioning the small matter of a global pandemic. So, thanks go to David Bowman and Beverley Randell, and to Tom, Amy, Lucy, Jonathan and all the other members of the team who have helped. Thanks also to Emma Tuck, whose perception and attention to detail have improved the prose immensely, and to all the others who read rough drafts and made suggestions.

Perhaps most importantly, though – if you're a teacher or leader who has read our work, used the materials, shared the books, spoken enthusiastically about VESPA, suggested the model to others, written research about it, completed a qualification based on it, requested that we visit to discuss the model further, thanked us for our newsletters, used our psychometric, shouted about us on social media or stayed behind to say hello after a training session – thank you.

Contents

Introduction

Introduction

We've been teaching for twenty-five years apiece, but for the last fifteen or so, we've also been building a body of work on another related project. Working with young people at Key Stage 3, 4 and 5, we've had one research question in our minds: *what are the characteristics and behaviours of successful students?*

When we began this project back in 2010, the whole thing was pretty rough and ready. We had some developing awareness of what we could see the highest performing students doing, but we were far from sure. When we watched them in class, as we often did, we saw them do things differently: they'd take more detailed notes, sit towards the front if given a choice, hand homework in early and request that it be checked through, keep their focus on the progress they'd made even when times were tough, or make a note of the kind of grades they wanted by the end of the course. Gradually, over the next four years, we continued to watch students, interview them, collect further behaviours and experiment with thematic groupings, so we could more easily codify what we were seeing.

What interested us back then – and still does now – was the potential for improving outcomes for all students by clarifying and democratising access to the tactics that high-performing students were using. It's a topic we're still obsessively investigating. Over the last decade and a half, we've spent lots of our time talking to students in the UK and beyond about things like:

» The struggles they face in their studies.

» The solutions they develop for those challenges.

» The revision methods they use.

» The strategies they have for staying positive and motivated when work is hard.

» The ways in which they organise their files of notes.

We also speak to teachers about their impressions of their learners to see if we've missed anything. What we've been trying to flesh out for all these years is our understanding of what exactly we should be telling our students to do differently when they study. This means avoiding survivorship bias: there's little point in gathering the habits of the most successful learners if those precise habits are also in evidence among the ones who fail. Research from academics around the world has been incredibly helpful, and you'll see a lot of it referenced in this book, but there's something particularly special about collecting primary data: impressions from real students doing real work. Every time we discover something new, some nugget of information or facet of behaviour that distinguishes the most successful, we try to write it up, turning it into a resource which makes that tactic learnable by others.

However, the characteristics and behaviours we've spent three books detailing took some years to come into focus. Back in 2010, all we had was a jumbled list of actions that typified the learners making the most progress. Whenever we were stumped by exam outcomes we didn't expect or by progress that had seemingly faltered, we'd dive deep into the student's behaviours. How had they behaved in and out of class? How had they approached their studies? What had been missing? We quickly realised that past performance didn't guarantee future performance; that a range of metacognitive factors played a significant role in determining the grades students achieved.

But we had a decision to make: what factors looked like they might be the most important? Which could we most easily change? The research was confusing. Some studies we read extolled the virtues of self-efficacy; others found links between time management and exam outcomes; still others made a case for confidence or conscientiousness as key characteristics.

Eventually, after four years of hard work, we finally arrived at a model that we thought accurately identified the most important behaviours we were seeing. It was the VESPA model, and its components are:

» **Vision.** Students who got great exam grades had a developing awareness of what success looked like for them. They had some sense of how education was going to be valuable, and had begun clarifying their aims and ambitions. They also had a stronger bias for action than others, tending towards doing rather than just ruminating.

» **Effort.** Successful students were outworking their peers, often significantly. Once we began to quantify effort, we quickly found high-performing students who were working four or five times harder in a typical week than those who underperformed. They were proactive setting themselves work rather than passively waiting for instructions.

» **Systems.** High-performing students organised their learning materials in a way that meant they understood the structure and content of the course; they knew where its edges were, what was on the syllabus and what wasn't. They also looked ahead, organised their time, completed work in multiple sittings and sequenced activities so they met deadlines.

» **Practice.** The students with the best grades revised differently. They began like the others did, rewriting their notes and checking study guides and textbooks, but soon after that they were designing study sessions in which they used the information they'd learned to solve problems under timed conditions. They operated at the edge of their ability and obsessed over the things they couldn't do rather than restudying the topics they felt confident about.

» **Attitude.** There was a psycho-emotional component to the success of the learners who made the most progress. They had developed habits of mind which promoted determination and tenacity; they felt they were in control of the grades they were going to get, saw feedback as a vehicle for further development, managed to stay positive when study was hard and maintained a belief that they were capable of even more improvement.

Little did we know, as we assembled this model at a comprehensive school in Greater Manchester back in the autumn of 2014, that 3,500 miles away in Canada, three researchers were beginning work on an experiment that was to discover something remarkably similar.

That same year, Associate Professor of Economics Graham Beattie began working alongside Jean-William Laliberté and Philip Oreopoulos to study a huge group of undergraduates at the University of Toronto (Beattie et al., 2016). Our contexts couldn't have been more different; while we were treading the corridors and classrooms of an urban comprehensive in the North of England, Beattie, Laliberté and Oreopoulos were working with students studying at Canada's most prestigious university.

Founded in 1827, the University of Toronto is something of a hallowed institution. Like some of the UK's oldest universities, it is composed of a series of semi-autonomous colleges. In 2023, the Times Higher Education Rankings graded Toronto as Canada's best university, standing at eighteenth worldwide* – sitting comfortably in the tranche just below Oxford, Harvard and Massachusetts Institute of Technology, alongside UCL, Cornell and New York University – although with a research profile that puts it comfortably in the world's top ten. In the year of the study, the average admissions grade of the students involved was 87% (Beattie et al., 2016, p. 8) – the UK equivalent of, let's say, an A* and two As at A level.

As the students arrived at university for the first time, no doubt excited to settle into their new accommodation, explore their new city and experience life at undergraduate level, the research team asked them to complete a one-to-two-hour 'warm-up exercise' – to fill out a series of questionnaires. These

* See https://www.timeshighereducation.com/world-university-rankings/2023/world-ranking.

questionnaires, the researchers informed the students, would be worth 2% of their final first-year mark and would involve simple, short prose answers to questions about 'procrastination, study habits, social identity, academic expectations, grit, risk aversion, time preference, [and] locus of control' (p. 3) as well as, for the subset we're interested in, levels of effort, persistence of interest, the ability to defer gratification and finally, a goal-setting exercise.

Just over three thousand students took part in the subset we'll discuss – a huge sample.

Once the three researchers had collected the data, they simply waited. At the end of the first year, all the undergraduate students had to complete an exam. The stakes were high: they had to pass to complete the first year successfully and progress to the second. A career in the classroom might lead us to believe that past performance equals future performance, and that the precise grades that students achieved before arriving at university might be the only predictor of success at this new level. Furthermore, we might think that, since the students had all done exceptionally well previously, there would be little issue with underperformance in the cohort.

That wasn't the case. Instead, there was a normal distribution curve of performance, with the highest performers averaging twice the marks of the lowest. The researchers chose two samples: the outliers at the top and bottom of the year. The 'performance gap between the two outlier groups [was] colossal,' they noted (p. 10). 'Divers' fell in the bottom 10% of their year group, averaging 40% in their exam and having to retake the test (every single diver had to be placed on probation at the end of the first year). 'Thrivers', by contrast, ended up in the top 10%, with an average score of 81%, outperforming most of their peers.

The research team then went back to the questionnaires of these two distinct groups to ask themselves whether the questionnaire responses collected in the first two weeks at university could have predicted exam performance many months later. First, though, they put a potential misconception to bed. Past exam performance was indeed a good indicator of whether a student would dive or thrive, but, 'When no demographics are included,' they noted – and here the italics are ours – '*less than 20% of the observed variation in college grades is explained by admission grades*' (p. 14).

So, what *did* determine the students who ended up in the two samples? The patterns they discovered are fascinating.

Vision played a part. Divers and thrivers set different types of goal; where thrivers focused on the process of learning and the purpose of acquiring a degree – the kinds of work they might end up doing or the real-world problems to which they would contribute solutions – divers had goals that specified levels of wealth or status. Thrivers had what we call 'do' goals; their language focused on active verbs – 'building' networks, 'solving' problems, 'working' at challenges, 'contributing' to teams – what the study called 'philanthropic goals' (p. 21). Divers, by contrast, had what we refer to as 'have' or 'be' goals; stative verbs about ownership such as 'having' a house or car or 'being' rich. The process of acquisition, and the associated work, wasn't part of the equation for divers; it was all about the outcome. Interestingly, the study suggested that the divers might have spent more time thinking about the future than the thrivers, but their goals didn't positively impact subsequent behaviour.

What else did the study discover? The researchers found that *effort* played a significant role in success, perhaps the most significant. Divers worked less hard than thrivers. 'Overall,' the study concludes, 'our findings suggest that effort (study hours) … is the key predictor to an exceptionally successful transition to college' (p. 17). Quite simply, thrivers were 'willing to study more hours per week to obtain the higher GPA [grade point average] they expect' (p. 21).

A student's ability to organise their time emerged as essential. Divers' *systems* for managing time and attention weren't as strong; so much so that they took much longer to submit their data back at the start of the academic year. Despite being fresh at university and no doubt eager to get off to a good start, they used the two weeks they'd been given to complete the questionnaires poorly and tended towards filling them in at the last minute. Their written responses had far higher incidences of words like 'procrastinate' and 'all-nighter' (p. 13).

The way students revised – their *practice* – played an important role too. Divers 'self-report cramming for exams' (p. 20), which suggests a set of approaches that emphasise the importance of quick, surface-level retention of material rather than steady, strategic year-long learning.

Finally, there were a series of *attitudinal* traits that emerged in written answers which suggested a difference between divers and thrivers. 'Discipline' was a descriptor thrivers used more often of themselves, as was 'responsibility,' and, interestingly, 'practice' – all words, the researchers conclude, 'which are indicative of conscientiousness' (p. 17).

They might have been conducting their study 3,500 miles away from us, and in a very different context, but if the researchers had wanted to find evidence of the five VESPA characteristics being predictors of academic success, they couldn't have done a much better job.

It's strange to think that we didn't know of this study at the time. In fact, we only came across it in 2020, six years after we'd developed the VESPA model and some years after we'd begun writing about it, beginning with *The A Level Mindset* in 2016, and followed by *The GCSE Mindset* in 2017 and *The Student Mindset* in 2018.

Even now, we feel a strange kinship with Beattie, Laliberté and Oreopoulos. Now and again, we'll check in with their Google scholar pages to see how they're getting on.

Embarrassing but true.

Using this book

This could be the first time you've read anything about the VESPA model – and that's fine. Or this might be the fourth book you've bought exploring the VESPA model – that's fine too.

The materials we include here are all entirely new and all written post-COVID-19. There are no activities that also appear in *The A Level Mindset*, *The GCSE Mindset* or *The Student Mindset*, and no activities that depend on the reading of those books to work effectively. If you're here for the first time, consider this as good an introduction to our work as any other book; and if you enjoy delivering the activities here, you've got just over eighty others waiting for you in our earlier publications. If you know the first eighty-or-so activities back to front, think of *The VESPA Handbook* as an expansion pack – forty new resources to play with.

Although our previous books have been distinguished by activities specifically attached to key stages, that isn't the case here. In our own classroom practice, since the publication of our books, we've found ourselves using the activities we enjoy the most and that, personally, we've found had the greatest impact with students regardless of their key stage. So, we've liberated you from that concept in this collection.

If you're a head of Year 9 wanting a curriculum of tutorial study to prepare students for their GCSE years, this book is for you. If you're a head of Year 11 looking for a series of resources that focus attention and encourage a greater commitment to out-of-class study, this book is for you. If you're a head of sixth form looking to improve the levels of proactive independent learning in your Year 13 cohort – well, you get the idea. Assistant heads charged with improving learning outcomes at particular key stages might get something from the material here, as might deputy heads keen to strengthen pastoral support or teaching and learning. We hope there's value here for as many of you as possible.

Each of the five main chapters of the book will take you through an element of the VESPA model. We've structured these chapters in the same way each time: first, we define what we mean by the element and then describe what we might see when it's lacking in learners. After that, we give you a brief overview of some of the most interesting research attached to the element and a summary of the findings. Finally – and perhaps most importantly – we give you a list of the behaviours that we see in students who have a strength in that area. We've collected these through interviews with students and teachers, and we've ensured that they're replicable. So, when you're supporting students, you can suggest – or have them pick – the behaviours you or they think they can incorporate into their studies.

Then we dive into the activities. There are eight for each of the VESPA headings, so forty in total. We have designed them to take about twenty or thirty minutes to deliver. Not all of them will suit your tastes, preferences or context, and that's completely normal; some will strike you as useful (we hope!), others might not. Some you might envisage delivering to large numbers of students via an assembly; others will strike you as deliverable to a tutor group or class; still others might look like they'll work in a seminar or coaching setting. We've tried to cover all bases, so pick and choose.

After the forty activities, we take you through a chapter on curriculum design. Some of you will consider the activities best suited to developing metacognition through tutorial programmes. That's certainly how we've used them, and the mini schemes of work we've designed all assume a pastoral context for delivery. But that doesn't mean it's the only way; some of our curricula would work just as well delivered in twenty-minute bursts in a classroom context. If that's the lens through which you see the material here, that's OK as well. We've spoken with staff who use the VESPA resources as a first-aid kit: when an issue arises in their class (a number of students miss a deadline, for example, or a posse stay behind to claim they don't know how to revise), the activities are ready and waiting to be delivered. Both approaches work – it will be what you're trying to achieve, and on what scale, that will determine how you use the material.

And, of course, you don't have to use our curriculum designs at all. Every organisation is different: some place an emphasis on systems, others feel their students need a big dose of vision. There's no requirement to balance out delivery so that every aspect of the model gets equal airtime, and there's certainly no obligation to approach each element of the model separately and in acronym order. When we're designing schemes, we'll often assess what we want to get out of a particular period of time – what messages we want to communicate, what ideas we want in the ether, what conversations and reflections we want our students to have – and then build something that helps us get there. You could ignore our suggestions and do the same!

We finish the book with a chapter exploring the power of the VESPA questionnaire. Thousands upon thousands of students have taken the psychometric test since it was first developed; it gives both students and staff a useful starting point for reflection and discussion about the role metacognitive skills play in the learning process. Coaching conversations are quickly elevated when both coach and coachee can refer to the reports generated by the questionnaire software. We provide some examples of what these reports look like and hear from five leaders who use the online psychometric questionnaire and associated resources to support their students.

Lastly, in the conclusion, we continue a tradition begun in our first book and followed in the others, by drawing together the main strands and concepts we've discussed in ten concluding observations.

So, whatever it is that interests you, whatever change you're trying to make and whatever ambitions you have for your learners, we think that there will be something useful for you here.

Good luck with your project!

If you have high control over the outcome, there's no need to have general goals – you can afford to get specific. But if you have low control over the outcome, general might be better.

1. Vision

Vision: the level of goal awareness and goal orientation shown by a student; their growing understanding of their reasons for studying, and their developing sense of what success might look like for them.

What Do We See When Vision is Low?

Like any of the metacognitive characteristics in the VESPA model, vision is not a fixed, unwavering element of personality. We can't dismiss low-vision students as permanently impossible to motivate. Students' levels of vision, goal orientation or dedication are malleable. They change in response to circumstances, culture, events in personal or family life, conversations, sudden epiphanies or exciting lessons.

When vision is missing, we'll see proxies for it that might include some or all of the following behaviours. Students might seem disengaged or bored. They might have little awareness or understanding of why education benefits them or what success might look like for them. They may have few or no ideas about how education opens doors to certain careers, or they might have no access to alumni programmes which clearly and persuasively show them where last year's students ended up. They might have begun to feel exasperated with themselves and others, envious of those who seem dedicated and feel the first tremors of a growing anxiety: what am I doing this for? Why are others enjoying this and I'm not? Is there something wrong with me? They might be firm believers in the passion myth; since they don't yet know that passion for something arrives as a result of growing mastery, they hunt around, convinced that if they could just find the one thing they're passionate about, everything will be OK again.

It's a complicated cocktail of difficult feelings. But we can help low-vision students navigate themselves through them.

Research Spotlight: What the Evidence Indicates

Let's focus on one important element of vision: goal setting. Evidence for goals positively impacting on performance is interesting to explore because not all research finds that students who set goals necessarily perform better.

For example, studies with young primary school pupils sometimes find little impact from goal setting, which we might expect when we consider their only gradually developing ability to defer gratification. But even with students of high school age, the research isn't unequivocal. One of the reasons could be the type of goal students set. For a quick – and, it's important to note, hugely simplified – summary of just some of the different types of goals students often set themselves, consider the following list. (The labels are all used in the literature around goal setting, but the student quotes and the order in which the types of goal are presented are ours.)

Achievement goals focus on seeking a positive outcome:

» Performance goals: 'I want to be the best in the class. If not, I want to be at least in the top three or beat a particular individual.'

» Mastery goals: 'I'm aiming to demonstrate an improvement in my ability to execute on this particular skill, which I've been reflecting on, tracking and practising.'

» Do-best goals: 'Regardless of the outcome, I want to feel as if I've done myself justice and feel a sense of satisfaction.'

» Challenge-seeking goals/personal bests: 'I know how I tend to perform in these situations and I have data to evidence where I'm up to. I'm aiming to use feedback, reflection and practice to achieve my highest score yet.'

Avoidance goals focus on averting a negative outcome:

» Performance-avoidance goals: 'I want to perform anonymously so that I don't stand out as in any way incompetent.'

» Mastery-avoidance goals: 'I know there's a specific way I tend to mess this up. I'm focusing on avoiding that error in my execution.'

» Failure-avoidance goals: 'I know what the pass mark is. I'm going to go into the exam focused on that, and just make sure I get over the line.'

Simply assessing these seven approaches to goal setting might have us thinking of specific students we've taught in the past. We might also have experience-based ideas about which goals are likely to positively impact on academic performance and which aren't. In case you're wondering, the research is constantly developing as more goal types are added to models. Two academics from the University of Lausanne summarise one aspect helpfully for us: 'Consistently in achievement goal research, pursuing performance-avoidance goals has been associated with a decrease in achievement' (Świątkowski and Dompnier, 2021, p. 1).

And, when it comes to the difference between two achievement goals – performance goals and mastery goals – we consistently see further interesting differences. One 2004 paper found that 'performance-oriented students tend to embrace surface learning [which is] characterized by more memorization and less effort. In contrast, deep learning, which frequently appears among student[s] who are mastery-oriented, probably lasts longer and raises the quality of students' learning' (Alhadabi and Karpinski, 2020, p. 2; see also Duff, 2004). Other studies find that mastery goals increase intrinsic motivation as well as reducing anxiety and improving enjoyment of learning (Greene et al., 2004; Ranellucci et al., 2015).

Hopefully, one thing is clear: simply having a goal isn't enough. We need to help students set goals that will work for them – encouraging them away from avoidance towards achievement and raising their levels of self-efficacy.

What else does the evidence tell us? Any exploration of goal setting takes us to the work of Professors Edwin Locke and Gary Latham who, from the 1970s and 1980s onwards, have explored goal-setting theory in several much referenced books and papers. Their focus is often on goal difficulty and performance. 'Hard goals,' they write, 'lead to greater effort and persistence than easy goals, assuming the goals are accepted' (Locke and Latham, 1990, p. 29). Specificity is also something that interests them; they spend time exploring, through meta-analyses, the power of specificity, concluding that 96%

of the studies analysed 'showed significant, or contingently significant effects in favour of specific, hard goals' (Locke and Latham, 1990, p. 30). In comparison, they report, subjects with do-best goals use less stringent standards to assess themselves and are therefore more likely to experience dips in performance.

The phrase 'assuming the goals are accepted' will surely catch the eye of any teacher. Working with students all the time, as we do, we're likely to have observed that the learner's psychological enrolment in the process of improvement is crucial to extracting greater levels of commitment.

Professor Andrew Martin's work at the University of New South Wales is interesting in this respect. He took eighty-nine students from both primary and secondary schools and put them through two maths exams a year apart, the first in August 2012 and the second in 2013. In preparation for the second test, forty-one of the students set themselves challenge-seeking personal best goals before the exam; the other forty-eight had a goal selected for them. Both groups were balanced as far as possible for gender, age and other demographics.

The goal-setting group were given a questionnaire asking them to outline their aims for the approaching test. They were provided with lots of possible goals and had the freedom to commit to whichever goals they wanted. Afterwards and separately, they were asked to set themselves a challenge-based personal-best goal with the following prompt: 'Last year you scored xx/40 in your mathematics test. Can we encourage you to set a Personal Best (PB) target for this year's mathematics test that is higher than last year's test?' (Martin and Elliot, 2015, p. 7). Once the student had chosen their own challenge goal, they were reminded regularly (by text) of this goal in the days running up to the test.

The second group were given the same questionnaire and had the chance to respond to the same goal options. Afterwards and separately, however, they were given a goal and were not reminded of their goal once it had been set.

Both groups received no teaching specific to the test, and the test they sat was not identical to the previous year's, but what the researchers call 'parallel' – that is, similar in structure and challenge (forty questions, a mix of multiple choice and short answers).

So, what happened? The group who had been given a goal scored 74% on test one, and a year later had slipped to 71%; a drop in performance was recorded across every subgroup. In the absence of test-specific teaching, we'd expect the attrition of time on memory and understanding to impact on outcomes, as well as the increased weariness and pragmatism that often come with the onset of adolescence. The group who had chosen their own personal-best goal fared batter. They scored 75% on test one, and a year later scored 78% – a statistically significant boost in performance that was replicated across every subgroup, despite facing the same challenges as the other group.

When We're Working with Students ...

Although the evidence indicates that challenging achievement goals which target specific improvements in performance with reference to previous outcomes and are chosen by the student are likely to yield the best academic performance, we might not start there. Why? Because a student who has never set themselves an academic goal – and there are plenty whose lack of agency and self-efficacy prevent goal setting – might need to begin with something simpler. Modelling the process of goal setting is a powerful place to start.

Here are a few approaches we've found useful.

1. Try beginning with a one-week do-best goal

We might ask the student to consider the week ahead. 'Where would you like to be by Friday? Let's picture the situation: you go into the weekend tired and ready for a break, but also feeling delighted that you've done your best and dealt with a number of issues. What might they be? What do we want to achieve in the next few days to make that happen?'

Try making the outcome as visual and visceral as you can. Encourage students to imagine what it would feel like to reach these goals – what a relaxed, stress-free weekend they would have and the things they could do with their time. Then conclude with two or three actions that are comfortably within their control. 'So, you're saying that tidying up your notes in English would make you feel much better. You also mentioned catching up on those missing notes in history. And you've also mentioned speaking to your teacher about that missing textbook. When might we try to schedule these jobs?'

2. Use a short-term checkpoint for a do-best goal

Here, we might refer to the organisation's short-term calendar: 'It's parents' evening in two weeks' time. Let's imagine what a great parents' evening would look like. What would your teachers be saying? What improvements might they mention? How might your parents respond? Wouldn't it be great to give them some good news!' Then discuss the possible actions that would close the gap between the current reality and the vividly imagined future state. 'What actions could we plan over the next two weeks? What might make a difference?' When we're dealing with these marginally increased time periods, we'll often suggest a midpoint check-up. 'So, by the end of this week, you'll be looking to have done this. Let's schedule a quick meeting so you can bring me up to date with what you've ticked off your list.'

3. Add a specific achievement goal, but choose a context where levels of control are high

We might introduce discussion of an achievement goal here, but select carefully. 'So, you'd like your test grades in science to improve. What scores are you getting at the moment? Are you entirely happy with those scores? If we decided to aim for something higher, what would be sensible?' Try to ascertain levels of control and likely success. We don't want students telling us they don't know why their scores are low or they haven't really got time to focus their attention in that direction. We're looking for learners to tell us, 'Yes, I know what my current scores are. I know I can do better. I just need to do more of …' Outcome Control (Activity 5) might help here. Once we're clear on a goal, we should attach actions associated with improved performance as above, and track them if necessary.

4. Introduce multiple achievement goals attached to a short- to medium-term checkpoint

At this stage, we might begin discussing a range of connected aims around a period of testing, an assessment week across a few subjects or a set of mock exams. 'Are there three or four subjects where you'd really like to make improvements? Which ones would they be, and why? What kind of improvements might you want to see?' Again, see if you can ascertain the extent to which the student has control over the outcome. 'Do you know what you need to do to improve, or does it all feel mysterious?' Introduce the idea of a personal best. 'What has your best result been so far? Why did it happen? If you were to try and beat that, what would you need to do?' Then, as above, attach actions.

5. Introduce and discuss more abstract, longer term goals when levels of self-efficacy have improved

Here, we might ask some of the questions we've wanted to from the start, but we've known that beginning with them, particularly with a student who has never set goals before, would result in confused shrugs and silence. 'Have you ever thought about what success looks like for you? Imagine it's results day, and you're opening that email and reading your exam results for the first time. What would have you punching the air?' Then, you might begin an exploration of the student's 'why'. 'Results like the ones you've just mentioned would open a lot of doors. Some of those doors might interest you, some might not. Can you give me an idea of which doors you'd want to explore further? Imagine you were only allowed to take one subject after your exams – just one door. Which would it be and why?' Record these hopes and aspirations, and then – you've guessed it – discuss the kinds of actions necessary for those outcomes to happen. Prioritise the actions and schedule the first one or two if you can. And remember, longer term goals need to be thriver goals, not diver goals (see Introduction).

Twenty High-Vision Behaviours

We've spent plenty of time with highly motivated and goal-oriented students with a clear vision for what success looks like. Whenever we find ourselves working with them, we aim to gather together their characteristics so we can share them with others. We always try to tease out replicable behaviours, so the language we use isn't abstract or slippery; rather, we want habits we can encourage others to add to their repertoire.

The lists under each element of the model aren't exhaustive, of course, but here are the twenty behaviours we see most regularly among high-vision students.

1 I have personal bests that I'm trying to beat when I submit new work.

2 I have a clear idea of what I need to know in order to understand everything well, so I ask the teacher to clarify tasks that I'm not 100% clear on.

3 I have begun researching how other people got to where they are.

4 I have imagined what a good set of exam results look like for me. I have written them down somewhere, like a commitment to myself.

5 I have mental lists of things I hope for, from small to big academic achievements.

6 I have started to find out about current affairs by reading a news site, watching TV news or choosing a documentary to watch.

7 I have thought about what good work looks like, and I'm aware of that as I work.

8 I know why education is important to me – I have thought it through, maybe even written it down.

9 I like to ask questions for clarification in lessons and make contributions, such as volunteering answers or offering opinions.

10 I often talk to my friends about my subjects, going over complicated topics or sharing enthusiasms.

11 I seek out extra material (textbooks, articles, handouts, revision sites) to deepen my understanding of a topic.

12 I set targets, like a grade or a certain type of feedback to work towards, often with a timeframe in mind.

13 I sometimes have another class member I compete against.

14 I take an interest in certain careers or courses and seek out video clips or online articles about them, just to see if they might be for me.

15 I try to get involved in school life, joining clubs, helping others and building relationships that will help me as I go along.

16 I want teachers to say good things about me at parents' evenings or in written reports, and work to make sure those things are more likely to happen.

17 I'm happy to watch a film or read a book chapter connected to my learning, so I can find out more and make connections.

18 If the teacher suggests an out-of-class activity or opportunity, I consider it.

19 My attendance and punctuality are very good, and I work to maintain them.

20 When entering a lesson, I'm focused and immediately look for the starter task.

How might a list like this be useful? Here's just one way in which it might change student behaviour.

Try a never/sometimes/always analysis

This approach is simple but effective. Encourage students to make three columns – 'never', 'sometimes' and 'always' – and to give themselves a tick depending on how often they do that behaviour. The 'nevers' become possibilities for them to consider. Not all of them will look possible or easy, but some might be immediate tweaks they can make to their studies.

1. Vision Activity: Diver Goals and Thriver Goals

Three researchers (from the University of Pittsburgh in the United States and Toronto in Canada) worked together to find out what made students in their first year of university particularly successful or unsuccessful (Beattie et al., 2016). They got three thousand students in the first two weeks of their university courses to fill out a questionnaire. They had all applied to study economics at degree level and had good college grades.

The questions asked them about how hard they planned to work, what their typical study routines were and, most importantly, to outline their hopes and dreams. It's this last section of the study that is particularly relevant to us in this activity. The questions the students had to answer were:

» What are your two most inspiring goals?

» What kind of person do you want to be later in life?

» What qualities do you admire in others?

A year later, the researchers took the students who had ended up in the top 10% of their year group and compared them with the students in the bottom 10%. There seemed to be some superficial differences at first, but what struck the researchers was the nature of the goals the students had set for themselves. The students at the top and the bottom had both set goals, but those goals were expressed very differently.

Here's a summary:

Bottom 10%	Top 10%
1 'be rich'	1 'build something'
2 'get rich quickly'	2 'I can contribute to the human advancement of …'
3 'being successful'	3 'I want to try something different'
4 'having so many successful businesses'	4 'fix people's problems'
5 'have my own company/have my own house and car'	5 'independent person who can deal with problems'
6 'receive a high level of education'	6 'working in the field of computer science'
7 'be an actuary'	7 'build a strong foundation to succeed'

One group of students – the ones on the left – had *diver goals*. These focused on 'being' or 'becoming' something – usually rich or having/receiving something – money, a house, a particular job, status or power. These were goals about an outcome, not a journey.

The other group had *thriver goals*. These placed emphasis on activity and a sense of purpose – building, contributing, trying, fixing or dealing with problems. These were goals that didn't specify an outcome but gave detail about a process or journey.

And the outcomes were clear. Those students with thriver goals were significantly more successful. They'd avoided procrastination and worked harder.

Here's a list of ten other goals set by the same students. Can you guess which were top 10% students and which were bottom 10% students? It's pretty easy once you see the patterns, but in case you need them we've snuck in the answers below.

1 'to enjoy working hard and working smart'

2 'to own a big company'

3 'to build my network, name and career'

4 'become a very rich guy'

5 'helping tackle space research to deal with overpopulation'

6 'be rich where I do not have to worry about running out of money'

7 'a person who changes the whole goddamn world and also can contribute to the whole society'

8 'to be a person like Bill Gates'

9 'to provide assistance to others in need of help and support'

10 'to be a successful businessman'*

* The odd-numbered goals were set by top 10% students and the even-numbered goals were set by bottom 10% students.

What Goals Do You Have?

There's nothing wrong with wanting wealth and riches. The problem comes when your goal is just about wealth and riches, and doesn't emphasise action – as if the wealth and riches are a magical outcome that just happens. Beattie et al. showed that students in the bottom 10% actually spent longer thinking about their futures than top 10% students did – *but* they were just dreaming about what it might be like to be a millionaire. They did less work than their peers.

So, instead frame your goal in terms of what you might want to *do*. Emphasise action – the journey or the process.

Try these starters to help:

» I want to build ...

» I want to help solve the problem of ...

» I want to tackle the issue of ...

» I want to develop skills such as ...

» I want to work every day in the ... industry.

» I want to deal with the issue of ...

» I want to help people ...

....

....

....

....

....

Remember, if you set goals like this, there's still every chance that you'll end up very wealthy and successful. You'll also have the advantage of knowing a little about how you're going to make a change in the world. It's a win-win situation.

2. Vision Activity: Sweet and Sour Summers

In a 2015 interview on Tim Ferriss' podcast, lawyer, investor and former Google employee Chris Sacca tells a story from his childhood (Ferriss, 2015). Once he was old enough to earn money, each summer his parents would make him work for most of the holidays. They wanted to teach him the value of hard work, life experience and the importance of looking after money. Here's the trick, though: they made him do two jobs per summer holiday.

The first few weeks would be on a job he wanted to do. The work was hard, but he had the advantage of being interested. These would be the 'sweet' weeks, where it was fun to go into work, good to hang out with colleagues and the day-to-day activities were engaging.

The second few weeks would be on a job he didn't want to do. Typically, Sacca says, it would be a job that didn't interest him. These would be the 'sour' weeks, where the work was hard and repetitive, often very boring. Sacca still uses the phrase 'sweet and sour summers' to describe these holiday jobs, and explains that it was these experiences that gave him huge advantages over regular students, who often had no life experience at all compared to him.

Let's imagine we had Chris Sacca's parents. It's a few weeks before our summer holiday and we're lining up our employment. We're about to make some phone calls and send some emails, asking for the chance to do some summer work. Make some choices here and populate the two lists below.

What would be among your best possible summer jobs, and what would be among your worst? (They should be real jobs, so no 'chocolate taster' or 'Netflix watcher' allowed!) You might want to start by considering our list – we've imagined forty organisations that you might find in a typical town or nearby city, all waiting for your phone call – but after that, add your own.

Advertiser/graphic designer running local campaigns, architect's office, art gallery exhibition organisation, beauty therapist, book publisher, bookstore, charitable/fundraising organisation, computer games company, dietician/health advisor, eco/environmental organisation, educational psychologist, electronics company, engineering firm, farming/agricultural organisation, fitness centre, gym or swimming pool, foreign aid company, laboratory researching and

developing new products, legal services/local courts, local library, local MP, local police force, local radio station, logistics company of long-distance lorry drivers, manufacturing company, media company – local newspapers, magazines and TV, media company – short films and animations, medical company developing vaccines, museum, music therapist/teacher, recording studio, pharmacy, photographer, pupil referral unit, retailer, science museum, software firm, tabletop/boardgames design firm, theatre, town planning and urban design firm, veterinary centre, web design company

Sweet	**Sour**
....	....
....	....
....	....
....	....
....	....

Now that you've completed your list, imagine you're about to compose an email or make a call asking for work from one of your sweet summer jobs. You've got a chance to include:

» An introduction to yourself and what your interests are.

» What you're hoping to get out of your summer work.

» Specific projects or parts of the work you'd love to be involved in.

Use the space below to make some notes about what you'd want to include in your introductory email.

....

....

....

....

....

Some things to consider

Are there any themes emerging from your imaginary job choices? Think about whether your sweet jobs have certain similarities, or do your sour jobs? These might be clues to pursue when you start thinking about how you want to earn your living in the future.

Finally, push yourself to imagine trying to get one of your sweet jobs. Is it possible? What employers near where you live might take you on? Is there someone to whom you could speak? You never know, there might be a future career waiting for you …

3. Vision Activity: Ikigai

Ikigai (pronounced i-kee-gai) is a Japanese concept. It's difficult to translate exactly, but it means a reason for being, including a sense of joy and purpose.

It's very unlikely that your schooling until now has encouraged you to reflect on your reason for being. We often think of education in terms of money and contribution to the economy; less 'What's your reason for being?' and more 'What job do you want?'

By contrast, we've found the concept of *ikigai* to be very liberating when talking with students because earning power is only one of four equal considerations on the table.

The four things you should consider are: what you love, what you're good at, what the world needs and what you can be paid for. Together they look like this:

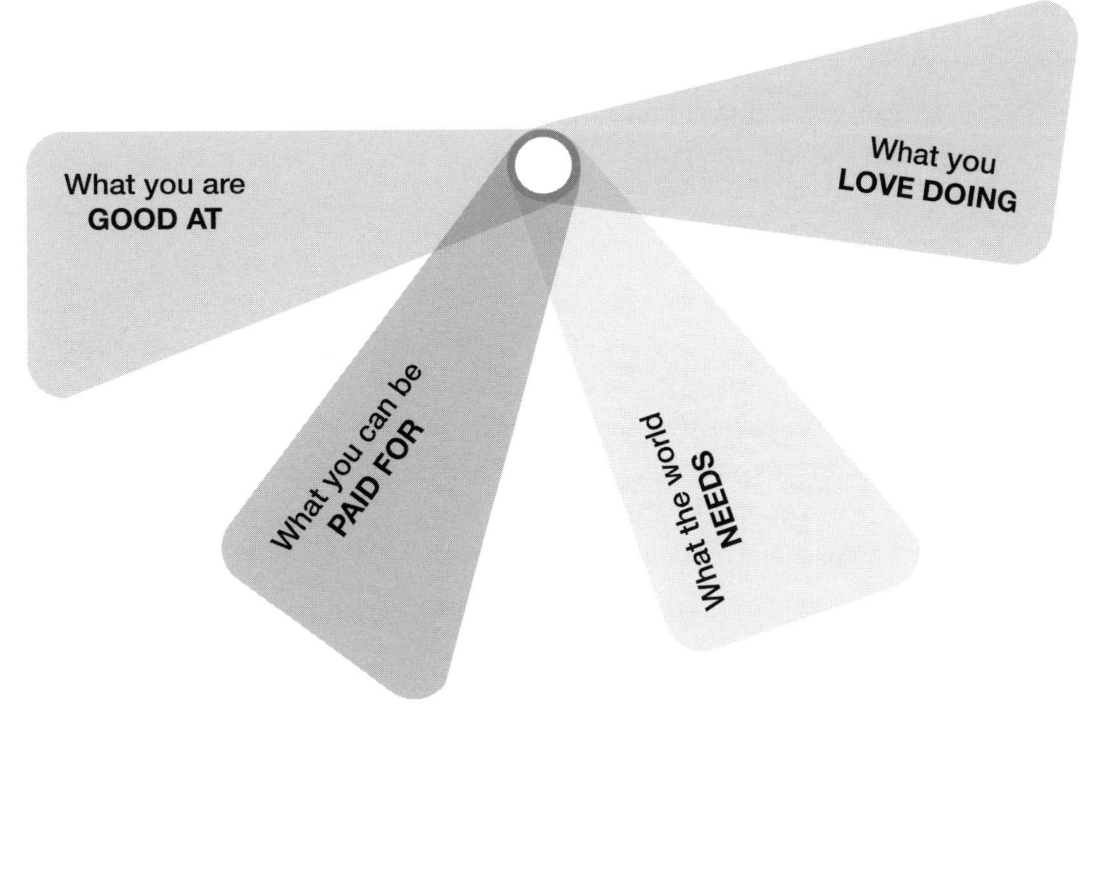

Of the four, two are *internal* – they're about you (what you love and what you're good at) and require some introspection and thinking. Two are *external* – about the world around you (what the world needs and what you can be paid for) and might require some research, discussion and further thought.

Not all four need to be equal. You need to find the balance that best expresses who you are, what you stand for and your values, beliefs, hopes and plans.

Here's one way of making this diagram work for you. Be ready to make two lists – one addressing the personal/internal questions and one addressing the external questions. We're going to suggest you go through six steps.

Step 1: Internal factors: List what you love

In this list, capture every interest you have. When are you happiest? What gets you excited? Be specific and exhaustive; precise rather than general. Make the list as long as possible. This may take more than one sitting as you capture everything you feel enthusiastic, curious and positive about.

Step 2: Internal factors: Add what you're good at

Extend the first list by adding things you're good at. Be kind to yourself – 'good at' doesn't mean 'the best at' or 'good relative to a world-class superstar'. It means good enough. Then see if there are connections between the things you love and the things you're good at. Some might be straightforward – you might love and be good at the same thing. Others might have looser connections. Shift things about, link them or scribble down additional ideas; turn your list into a vast interconnected mess of thoughts and ideas.

Step 3: Let it rest

Set your list aside. The chances are that it will look chaotic, so you'll need some time for it to percolate into your subconscious, where your brain can begin to make some sense of it. Then return and rework it.

Step 4: External factors: What can you be paid for?

Take your list of passions and strengths and begin to add your external factors over the top. You might use a highlighter, sticky notes or coloured pens, if that floats your boat. Of the items on the list, what can you be paid for? And how important is that money to you? Freedom, flexibility, creativity, autonomy, risk, challenge – all these things might be more important to you than cash.

Step 5: External factors: What does the world need more of?

Architects? Insurance advisors? Graphic novelists? Physiotherapists? Teachers? Soldiers? You have to make these judgements; they come from your experiences and world view. One person's roster will look very different to another's, and there's nothing wrong with that.

Look at your crazy list and add a final layer – what's already there that the world needs more of?

Step 6: Let it rest

From all the noise, you'll start to see clear themes emerging. You're not necessarily looking for a sudden specific job idea; instead, look out for repeated patterns.

These are the clues to pursue as you study.

4. Vision Activity: A Question of Money

Many of our hopes and dreams centre around money – getting it, having it, keeping hold of it. In 2010, two researchers – one a Nobel Memorial Prize winner – began exploring whether there was a strong link between someone's earnings and their happiness. They asked thousands of people questions about how happy they felt on a scale of 1–10, how stressed they felt and if they ever felt low. Then they organised those people according to the money they earned.

Did the richer ones feel happier? Yes … for a while, but once people's earnings hit around US$50,000 a year, happiness levelled off. More money after that had almost no effect (Kahneman and Deaton, 2010).

So, do other things affect happiness? Well, it turns out that, yes, there are other factors that lead to a well-lived working life. Pay is just one element; others might be freedom, the power to take decisions, creativity, a sense of purpose, belonging, optimism and teamwork.

Which Ones Might Matter to You?

In this thought experiment, we're going to imagine you've got a job that pays you very well. You can buy everything you need and you have no money worries.

So, given that, what would be important to you in this job? Of the thirty possibilities we've suggested here either (1) choose your top three or top five, (2) put a top ten in order of preference or (3) put all thirty in order of importance to you.

1 To face unfamiliar situations and improvise solutions in the moment.

2 To organise your own day on your own terms.

3 To be making a difference to people's health, well-being or happiness.

4 To be creative, producing new and original content.

5 To have status, power and expertise.

6 To solve problems for others, improving their lives.

7 To have a safe role, a job for life with no threat of ever being made redundant.

8 To wake early to an alarm clock and be up and active before everyone else.

9 To wake up every day excited for the day's work ahead.

10 To be finished at 5pm and not think about work until the next morning.

11 To be travelling from place to place.

12 To work in the same place each day, with the same commute and same workspace.

13 To develop new skills through practice and feedback.

14 To share your enthusiasm for something you're passionate about.

15 To have time to laugh and joke; to not take work seriously.

16 To lead others (making decisions about who does what).

17 To have someone else make all the decisions and tell you what to do.

18 To use your hands to practically build, maintain or fix something.

19 To be operating in a high-stakes, high-pressure environment.

20 To lead a low-stakes, stress-free life doing something unimportant.

21 To be in a busy, bustling atmosphere with music, activity and conversation.

22 To have predictable working hours with a set start and finish time.

23 To have a list of predictable tasks – every day roughly the same.

24 To stay late into the night, still focused long after others have gone home.

25 To be active, moving, physical – to be away from a desk.

26 To have a space of your own and projects you complete entirely by yourself.

27 To be helping to change people's opinions, attitudes and behaviours.

28 To dress however you want.

29 To respond to crises and emergencies as and when they come up.

30 To have every day different.

Now take a moment to see if there are any we've missed off our list that are important to you.

Where Might Money Fit In?

Now you've got a list of preferences, we'd like you to consider exactly where money might fit in. Using the space below, see if you can add some of the characteristics from the list above to the three columns.

I would be happy with lower pay as long as the job had …	As long as I had really decent pay I would put up with …	Regardless of the pay, I could never put up with …
....	....	....
....	....	....
....	....	....
....	....	....
....	....	....
....	....	....

Rather than designing a work life that pays well but we're desperate to get out of, we should perhaps be trying to design work lives that energise and excite us.

What themes about work seem to be emerging for you?

5. Vision Activity: Outcome Control

One classic piece of goal-setting advice is to be *specific* with your goals. The more specific the goal, the better, people often say. And this is true up to a point. But what if your goal is to be a lifestyle influencer with two million subscribers and an annual turnover of £100k? That's specific, but it doesn't mean it's more likely to happen. Here's a really ridiculous example: what if your goal is to be principal clarinettist for the New York Philharmonic? There's only one of those. That's a goal so specific that there's literally only a single slot available in the whole world.

So, being specific isn't everything. We also have to consider the *control* we have over the outcome.

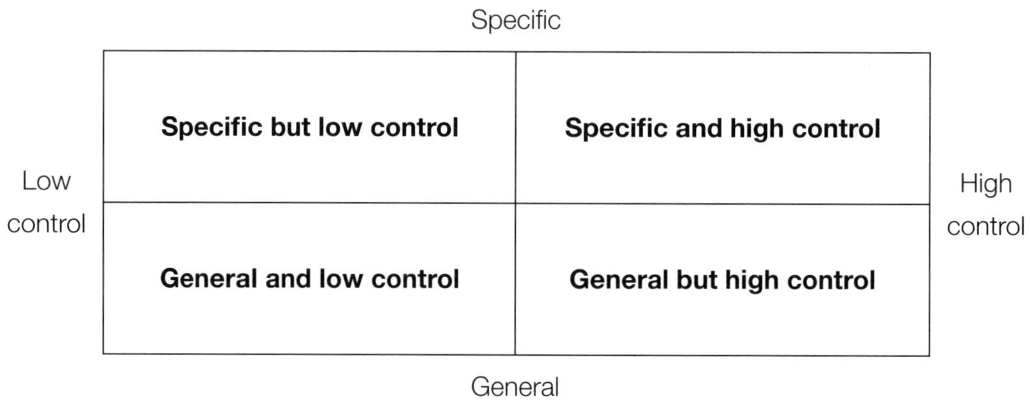

	Specific		
Low control	**Specific but low control**	**Specific and high control**	High control
	General and low control	**General but high control**	
	General		

These four quadrants might look complicated, but just take a moment to consider them again.

In the top left is a specific goal we have little control over ('Become top scorer for Arsenal and retire a multimillionaire at the age of 35').

In the bottom left is a general goal we have no control over ('Just be super famous').

In the top right we have a specific goal we can control ('Aim to beat my personal best in the next maths test').

Finally, in the bottom right, we have a general goal we have control over ('Just get some decent grades this summer').

Now is a good time to reflect and make some choices:

» Of these four types of goal, are some better than others, in your opinion?

» What kind of goals do you typically set for yourself?

» Are the types of goals you are setting yourself helpful? Possible?

» Do these types of goal serve different purposes? Are some just dreams we use to keep ourselves cheerful when we're down?

Now that you've had a moment to think your way through the idea of outcome control, let's try and establish a couple of simple rules.

Rule 1: If you have high control over the outcome, there's no need to have general goals.

You can afford to get specific. So, if you have a goal in the bottom right ('general but high control'), change it so that it's in the top right ('specific and high control'). You're in control of what exam results you get, so instead of thinking, 'I'd be happy with a few decent grades,' make your goal *more specific.* Have a go now!

Rule 2: If you have low control over the outcome, general might be better than specific.

If you have a goal that's in the top left ('specific but low control'), think about how you might move it towards the bottom left ('general and low control'). You're not in complete control of whether you end up a movie actor or not – there are a lot of factors at play and very few spaces to fill – so instead of thinking, 'I'm going to be a major Hollywood star,' make your goal more *general.* Have a go now!

A Four-Step Goal-Setting Activity

If you've never really set a goal before, here's a chance to try setting an academic goal that fits into the top right of the quadrant. You have a *high level of control* over the outcome –

remember, you're going to determine what grades you end up with – so you can afford to be *specific*. Have a go!

1 Choose a subject:

....

2 Choose a piece of work coming up (a homework you have to hand in, a submission or an upcoming test):

....

3 Choose a specific outcome you want (a mark, a percentage score, a grade or certain type of feedback):

....

....

4 List three things you could do to make the outcome you want more likely:

....

....

....

6. Vision Activity: The Paths Are Well-Lit

Whatever it is you want to achieve, the chances are that someone else has already managed to do it. Of course, that doesn't stop it feeling impossible sometimes. We might look at an amazing student who has got a place at a university we'd love to attend and think, 'Yeah, but that can't be me.'

But perhaps it can … if we somehow throw some light on the path they took. In this activity, we attempt to light up the pathway ahead using an activity that we've adapted from Cal Newport's book, *How To Be a High School Superstar* (2010, p. 225).

Newport uses the phrase 'innovation map' to describe a visual guide showing the steps someone takes to achieve something. Newport suggests there are three stages to each cycle of progress; we've adapted them here.

1 A trigger event: The student takes *an initial action*, which leads to …

2 An opportunity: *a brave and repeated action that results in an accomplishment*, which then leads to …

3 Responsibilities: *a series of actions that need to be regularly completed* and which give the student valuable experience.

Have a look at the example below. (We've filled this one out ourselves based on a combination of students with whom we've worked.)

Student: Joe

Achievement: Got a place on a journalism degree because of a great portfolio of work, then went on to write for the sports pages of a national newspaper.

Pathway – part 1

Trigger event	I discussed journalism with a teacher – they suggested I try to write a match report for a local non-league football team.
Opportunity	I got in touch with the club secretary via the team's website. I had to email him three or four times until he agreed to meet me. I went to the club and explained what I'd like to do. He agreed I could write up a match report for the club's website.
Responsibilities	I attended the match, took photographs and used the voice memo on my phone to remind myself of the main action. I wrote up the piece, asked a teacher to check it and then submitted it. The club published it on their website. I asked if I could do another and they said yes. After I'd done three match reports, they asked if I could report on every home game and, of course, I agreed!

By the end of the first part of the pathway, the student is in a really good position – and happens to be in the right place at the right time for the next cycle to happen. (It looks like luck, but of course it isn't.)

Pathway – part 2

Trigger event	I was asked to do a piece on non-league football for the local newspaper. They'd heard of me because I'd been doing the match reports for the non-league team, and I'd also started my own blog. I said yes and asked if I could visit the offices of the paper. They agreed.
Opportunity	I made sure I talked to the staff and looked really enthusiastic when I visited. I completed the piece as they requested, asked my teachers to check it over and then submitted it. They printed it! It was just a short piece but I had my first article in print. I suggested a couple of ideas for other pieces I could do. They agreed to think about it, so I kept on at them!
Responsibilities	I read a lot of sports journalism and kept a notebook of ideas for other articles. I knew from meeting the staff at the local paper that they liked small local stories, so I kept looking for things that might interest them. I had written three more pieces for them by the winter of Year 13. When I applied to university, I was the only one who brought printed newspaper articles along with me. The interview went really well and I got the place.

By using a table like this, we're beginning to see the steps taken by those who have gone before, and we're starting to see how they got themselves into positions that meant they were well-placed for other things to happen to them. Life is a series of cycles like this, with opportunities leading to more opportunities. The impossible is starting to look a lot more possible …

Now it's your turn!

1 Choose a student who's achieved something you'd like to achieve and interview them. Ask for half an hour of their time, and perhaps even show them the example above.

2 Complete the interview. It might feel a bit awkward, but just think of yourself as a journalist trying to find out the story of someone's success. It might be worth asking if you can record the discussion so you can listen back to it later.

3 Once you've got your conversation, try to make sense of it. The answers might have come out in a jumbled way. See if you can start decoding what it was they did and in what order.

Trigger event	....
Opportunity	....
Responsibilities	....

By the end (hopefully) you will have a well-lit path and know what you need to do next. Now the challenge is to be brave and begin your journey. Good luck!

7. Vision Activity: Twenty Questions (Part Two)*

We all know that the dreaded question, 'What do you want to be?' – often asked by parents, friends and family members – can feel impossible to answer. It's such an abstract and slippery question. For a start, we don't have enough information and answering it is often embarrassing. It's so much easier just to say, 'I don't know.'

We've found it's often useful to ignore big questions like, 'What do you want to be?' and answer lots of small questions instead. That way, we can observe the bigger picture that starts to emerge as we answer the smaller questions.

The following questions have been tested with students and seem to be ones that open up some positive thinking. We can't promise that they'll work for you; all we know is that they've worked for others.

You might not like them all – that's OK too. Aim to answer *two or three from each group of five* – and make notes! Record your ideas and see what begins to materialise.

Group 1: Study

1 Think of a friend who isn't doing the subjects you are. What enjoyable class would you ask them to sit in on to show them what they're missing?

2 If you wanted to persuade a younger pupil about one subject you take, what would you say are its strengths?

3 If you could only take one subject – and it lasted all week with detailed classes – what would it be, and what topics would you dive deeper into?

4 If you could specify the homework given to you, what kind of tasks might you ask for?

5 What topic (from a class or from your own life) do you know so well that you could teach a thirty-minute lesson on it without much preparation?

* For Twenty Questions (Part One), see Activity 1 in *The A Level Mindset*.

Group 2: Extracurricular activities

6 If you were in solitary confinement for a whole month, what activity might you do or learn to do to keep yourself sane?

7 List three clubs you used to attend after primary/secondary school. What are your memories of them? Now imagine you had to set up and run a club for younger pupils. What would it be about?

8 What hypothetical club, group or team might you feel most at home in?

9 What activity or interest did you think you might grow out of but haven't?

10 What is an activity or interest that other people seem obsessed with but you just can't see the point of? Is there something that interests you that others might not understand?

Group 3: Hypothetical questions – work and money

11 If you were a billionaire, what would you spend your money on once you'd bought yourself everything you'd ever wanted? Now imagine that you had no family. Who would you leave all that money to at the end of your life, and why?

12 If you had a million pounds, what might you do with it to positively impact the most people?

13 What kind of work are you absolutely determined *not* to do for a living?

14 If all jobs had the same pay and the same working hours, what job would you pick?

15 What problem(s) do you see in the world around you that you might like to help solve?

Group 4: Hypothetical questions – time

16 If an extra day of the week was created, and it had to be for 'improving your future', what activities might you plan to do?

17 What one thing have you been meaning to get around to but haven't yet? Is there something you regret not starting when you were younger?

18 What ingredients make a good life?

19 What would you like to be remembered for?

20 Imagine you're at the end of your working life. What would you regret not trying to achieve?

Now you've got some scribbled thoughts, take a step back and see what your answers look like:

» Are any themes beginning to become clear?

» Are you noticing patterns that you perhaps hadn't seen before?

» Have the questions helped to clarify something?

Don't worry if not. Sometimes activities like this trigger a number of thoughts, and you need time to consider them carefully before new certainties emerge.

Consider revisiting the questions again later; our answers often change as the year goes on.

8. Vision Activity: Lifestyle Envy versus Job Envy

We were once working with a student who'd always admitted to us that he never really knew what career he wanted. Not having any particular ambitions, he went off to university to study a subject he enjoyed. Then, two years later, he came back and told us he knew *exactly* what he wanted to do with his life. The realisation, he explained, had come in just one conversation.

We were shocked and fascinated. *What could have happened in a single conversation that suddenly made his ambitions so clear?*

He described the moment. He'd been talking to a classmate at university, and she had told him she'd just got a summer job. And the more she described this job, the more envious he felt. By the end, he was – to use his words – 'insanely jealous'. That was when he knew. He wanted that job too. He'd accidentally stumbled across the career he needed to pursue.

Ever since then, we've used this thought experiment to encourage others to put themselves in his shoes, giving them the scenario of a friend who shares some news about a job.

What kind of lucky break would make you envious?

We'd like you to try this thought experiment. You must imagine a friend telling you about a new opportunity they're about to take up. They're excited, and they're describing to you what it is they're about to begin doing. And the more you listen, the more you become 'insanely jealous'.

Here's the crucial bit: it doesn't need to be a super-specific job – you can keep it pretty general. We don't need the whole picture to make total sense, so don't limit your thinking or stop because it doesn't sound realistic. Just record exactly the kinds of things that would get the envy flowing.

Record your thoughts in the box below and use the ideas on the right if you need them:

	Think about: » Working hours. » Working conditions. » A typical working day. » Place of work. » The kinds of tasks and responsibilities. » Rewards on offer. » Further opportunities and chances that might follow. » Status.

Now consider all the things that have made you envious and separate them into two groups. Group 1 we'll call 'lifestyle envy' – these are all the things *outside of the job itself* (the amount of time off, the pay, the holidays). The other we'll call 'job envy' – all the things that have made you envious about *doing the work itself*.

Lifestyle envy	**Job envy**
....	....
....	....
....	....
....	....
....	....
....	....
....	....
....	....
....	....
....	....

If you find that your *lifestyle envy* column is full but the *job envy* column is empty – don't worry. This happens to us all sometimes; we can all get confused between lifestyle and job. We've seen students pursue a job or career because of the lifestyle they imagine it will give them, not because of the work itself. Like the student who applies to be a lawyer because they've seen legal dramas on TV and the after-work parties look glamorous and attractive. Or the student who wants to become an archaeologist because they imagine the travelling will be exciting, but haven't thought about the hours of back-breaking digging in the pouring rain. Or the student applying to be a teacher because 'the holidays are great'.

These decisions don't always make for a happy working life. To be truly content, it must be the work itself that is meaningful and important to you. So, if you've not written anything in the job envy column have a go at the activity again, this time focusing on what kind of work would make you envious. Keep it broad and general if it helps.

What themes are important to you? Ignore the left-hand column and have a look at the patterns emerging in the right-hand column. What qualities do you want in a job? Try turning it into a short paragraph of just a few sentences. If you don't know how to begin, try starting with, 'I'd like a job that allows me to …'

And, remember, focus on the nature of the work itself, not the lifestyle elements around it!

The problem is not that low-effort students can't work harder; it's that they might not know how, or that each time they try, they come up against seemingly insurmountable obstacles.

2. Effort

Effort: the hours of both reactive and proactive work students complete in and out of class; the levels of engagement, energy and commitment they dedicate to the process of learning.

What Do We See When Effort is Low?

Like any of the metacognitive characteristics in the VESPA model, effort is malleable. We absolutely must not write off low-effort students as permanently 'lazy' or 'apathetic'; levels of effort can easily change. The problem is not that low-effort students can't work harder; it's that they might not know how or that each time they try, they come up against seemingly insurmountable obstacles. We'd go as far as saying that all the low-effort students we've ever worked with have wanted to be more successful. They might be having significant difficulties, but none of them have wholly dedicated themselves to destroying their academic careers.

When effort is missing, we'll see proxies that might include some or all of the following behaviours. Students have habitualised low levels of effort for many years and have long since lost touch with what high-effort students do; they might genuinely have no idea that high-effort students set themselves work and are shocked to hear it. Because of their focus on reactive work completed in response to teacher instruction, they may baulk at being asked to complete extra study, claiming, 'I'm all caught up.' They may describe themselves as lazy because, after years of procrastination, it's a label they feel describes the person they've become; that they deserve it and that it can't be fixed. They might be addicted to what Cal Newport (2022) refers to as 'hyper-palatable digital distraction', and developed habits around screen use that have eroded their ability to concentrate to such an extent that they rarely sustain their focus beyond the first two or three seconds of each TikTok video. They might subconsciously self-sabotage, choosing to study in spaces where distraction is more likely. Finally, they may fall victim to procrastination because they don't plan study sessions or work in short sprints.

It's a difficult knot to unpick, but we can help using a series of simple and easily modelled activities. First, though, the research.

Research Spotlight: What the Evidence Indicates

Studies looking at effort are always fascinating. Researchers must untangle effort from a range of other factors and have difficulties in terms of exactly how they're going to measure it – objectively (the number of hours a week students claim to be working) or subjectively (the feelings of expending effort in order to challenge oneself to improve).

Despite these complexities, there are some thought-provoking findings. An interesting place to start might be the work of Xin Jin, a psychologist at the Free University in Berlin. In a 2023 study, thousands of Chinese students were analysed according to the levels of effort they put into their studies, both objectively (in hours) and subjectively (via a questionnaire asking them to reflect on the energy they expended tackling tricky topics). The scores they received on tests across the academic year were also collected. The results were unequivocal: 'effort matters for academic performance' (Jin, 2023, p. 11). After controlling for other effects, Jin found, 'On average, students who put in a more subjective effort achieve 12.7% higher scores than those who put in less effort. Furthermore, increasing study time by 1 h[our] is associated with a 3% increase in scores' (Jin, 2023, p. 8).

What about other studies? Michelle Richardson and her team at UCL completed a meta-analysis synthesising thirteen years of research into the factors that determine academic outcomes at university – including over two hundred data sets – and concluded that 'effort regulation' plays a hugely important role in determining grades, beaten only by self-efficacy as a predictor of exam success (Richardson et al., 2012).

Then there's the work of William Rau, emeritus professor of sociology at Illinois State University. His research also looked at effort among undergraduates; he collected hours worked – objective effort – and attempted to link it with academic outcomes. The correlation he found wasn't exact, but rather than this undermining the case for increased effort, his work reveals something fascinating. 'Initially, an increase in studying has little effect,' he observes, noting that as students move from 'zero to two hours a week' into the 'three to eight hours a week' group, there is only a very small impact on test results; in some cases it even goes down. That is, until the figure of fourteen hours a week is reached, and then, 'GPA [grade point average] jumps dramatically … and continues to increase', all the way up to twenty-seven hours a week, the highest level of effort recorded – which is, of course, correlated with the highest test scores too (Rau and Durand, 2000, p. 26). The fourteen-hour mark, Rau speculates, could be the point at which ad hoc cramming stops being part of the effort equation and, instead, we have systematic and steady weekly preparation instead.

Finally, we should consider Dr Sanne van Herpen's work at the University of Rotterdam. Van Herpen's team examined why some students do particularly well in their first-year undergraduate studies, while others drop out of university altogether. Could it be that they find the location problematic as they realise they don't like the organisation they've chosen to study with? Is it that their levels of confidence aren't high enough? Or does the amount of effort they put into their studies play a role? Unsurprisingly, it is effort that emerges as a crucial factor: raised effort means an increased chance of passing the first-year course and a significantly decreased chance that a student drops out. 'Effort seems to have a long-term effect on academic performance,' the researchers conclude, 'even during a period when students change school environment'. They go on to suggest that 'Secondary education staff could stimulate effortful learning behaviour in addition to performance behaviour when preparing students for university' (van Herpen et al., 2017, pp. 14, 15).

When We're Working with Students …

Simply urging students to 'work harder', 'pull your socks up' or 'put a shift in' has very little effect. If you've been low effort for several months or years, and you've normalised those levels of effort by making friends with students who put in similar levels, you no longer know what higher levels of effort look or feel like.

And those first epiphanies can be painful. We've done many a focus group where students write down a response to our standard effort question ('Can you give an estimate of how many hours' work, including homework, you completed last week?') on a sticky note. We've done it so often now that we can make pretty accurate predictions about what we're going to hear. (If you ask a focus group of Year 12s in a comprehensive school sixth form during half term two, you might get a lowest answer of something like one to two hours and a highest of something like fourteen to sixteen hours.)

When we ask all the students present to share their number and describe what they're doing with their time, low-effort students are often flabbergasted. ('*What?* Twelve hours? How? *What are you doing*?') Because they're entirely reactive, and get their homework done quickly to a standard just high enough to avoid a penalty, low-effort students naturally assume that's what others do too. Presented with the figure of twelve hours – or indeed twenty, the number of hours we hear most regularly from high-performing Year 13 students in terms two and three – they can only assume these students are simply doing their homework really slowly. The idea that they might be working proactively is entirely new.

So, what can we do? Here are some of the principles and approaches we've found useful.

1. Quantify and describe what higher levels of effort look like

It's tough getting students from low to high effort, partly because it has to happen gradually over a period of time and so needs a focus. It's worked best for us when we attach effort to certain outcomes. One example: we were supporting a large group of students who wanted to study medicine or dentistry at university, but many of them weren't working in the way we knew they needed to. We began interviewing students who'd successfully secured places on these courses and asking them our effort question. Not only that, but we also had lists of the kind of things they'd done with their time while studying. So, we had handouts telling aspiring medics: 'The Year 13 students who made it before you did between twenty-two and thirty hours of study outside of class in the final run-up to their exams. They tended to focus on …' We could also provide a list of proactive study strategies they'd habitualised. The same goes for Year 11s who made it onto challenging combinations of A levels: 'The students who made it onto maths, further maths and chemistry last year prepared for their exams in the following ways …'

2. Reward effort itself rather than waiting for the outcomes associated with effort

It's hard to change the way you study, and it's harder still when your teachers don't notice you're trying to change. We've had great success over the years designing mini challenges with rewards attached. Below is the text of an email we showed students at the beginning of one such project – a six-week focus on increasing effort. 'Anyone who really engages with the challenge gets this email home,' we told them. They studied the text of the email at the start of the project and were encouraged to visualise the consequences of their parents receiving it.

> **As I'm sure you know, at [level of study or course] success is the result of effort. Students who put in the hours, working diligently and optimistically, are the ones who do best. With this in mind, I have been keen to praise those students who have worked really hard over the last six weeks or so. [Name] has certainly been one of those students this half term, and I have made it clear how impressed I've been. Could I ask you to reinforce this praise at home? A positive word, a gesture or a small reward might really help to encourage this approach to study for next half term as well.**

It worked spectacularly well!

3. Low-effort students are very rarely lazy, even if they describe themselves as so

Most students want to improve; they know they need to do better, but they find it hard to change. One of the main issues we see is an unhealthy relationship with distraction. If it isn't gaming, it's mindless scrolling or social media. Short bursts of screen-free study are the solution here. Use Twenty-Five Minute Sprints (Activity 26 in *The GCSE Mindset*) and sequence a week of twenty-five minute distraction-free study sessions. (Start with twelve to fifteen minutes if low-effort students find twenty-five too much; we often need to train and build the muscle of concentration gradually.) Try what we call the 'Five Hundred Minutes Challenge' – very simply, it's a week of twenty twenty-five-minute screen-free study sessions (20 x 25 = 500) with a reward at the end.

4. The fear of work is worse than the work itself

Low-effort students fall prey to prevarication and procrastination because they conceive of their work as involving extended periods of extreme discomfort. Instead, encourage short, pain-free bursts of work with clear boundaries. In The Ten Minute Rule (Activity 14 in *The A Level Mindset*), we suggest that students tell themselves, 'I'm just going to do ten minutes of work.' One of two things happen: they either do ten minutes of work and stop (in which case they've done ten minutes more than they would have ordinarily) or they forget the time, become absorbed and carry on for longer.

5. Remember the power of compounding and of fresh starts

Several of the effort activities that follow emphasise a little-and-often approach. The Clarity Countdown (Activity 15) helps students to avoid the gradually compounding sense of dread that comes with falling further and further behind. Red Flag Rescue Plans (Activity 16) asks them to consider the behaviours that typify the beginnings of a period of slippage. Both activities work well when connected to a fresh start. Working with students to devise a new plan or beginning is always a powerful way to change behaviour. This new beginning doesn't need to be immediate; it often works well to plan it ahead of time with learners. 'So, looking ahead, next Wednesday is the big day – the clean slate and the fresh start. Let's remind ourselves – what are we doing differently from next Wednesday onwards? What's it going to look like?' (We often choose a mid-week start rather than a Monday, which means students only have to operate at their new levels of effort and engagement for two or three days before getting a break.)

Twenty High-Effort Behaviours

Whenever we find ourselves working with a learner who demonstrates high levels of proactive effort, we try to identify and gather their key behaviours so we can share them with others. We look for those habits and strategies we can model and demonstrate; the ones that go beyond 'put the hours in' towards small and manageable adjustments that other students can experiment with and add to their working weeks.

The lists under each element of the model aren't exhaustive, of course. Here are the twenty behaviours we see most regularly among high-effort students.

1 I can increase periods of concentration if I have to; I know what my main distractions are and how to turn them off so I can focus.

2 I challenge myself when studying topics I am not familiar with, working carefully to understand them and then revisiting them for checks more often.

3 I complete draft work in advance and ask the teacher to take a quick look at

it, so I can make any changes before the real deadline.

4 I don't mind putting in some work over the weekend reviewing difficult work or going through a study guide or website to stay on top of things.

5 I generally know in advance what I plan to achieve in a study session. Rather than start it and just hope, I break it down into parts and plan what each part looks like.

6 I have an out-of-school routine for homework – doing it when I get home or at the same time each day to ensure my effort isn't wasted.

7 I often ask about the success criteria/ requirements of the task, so I'm more likely to produce quality work.

8 I often ask myself, 'What can I also do?' and create my own extension criteria, aiming to impress my teacher by giving more than they asked for.

9 I often go looking for problems – seeking out topics I find hard and listing the questions I want to discuss with my teacher.

10 I often go over work one last time before handing it in, just to check it's as good as I can make it.

11 I often go the extra mile to complete work to a really high standard, asking myself, 'What would this look like if it were excellent?'

12 I set myself little tasks, like reading over the previous week's notes, checking a study guide or textbook, or trying to find the answer to things I don't understand.

13 I sometimes approach teachers and ask for suggestions for additional resources or reading recommendations.

14 I sometimes speak to teachers or students to check I know what to do before I start, to ensure my effort is targeted wisely.

15 I try to see the value in the work my teachers set and explain to myself why it's important, even if I sometimes have to persuade myself.

16 I watch what higher achieving students do in class and sometimes steal behaviours from them.

17 I work without screens, headphones or alerts, switching everything off so it's just me and the task.

18 If I'm given a choice of homeworks, I sometimes do both.

19 Sometimes I look ahead to what we're studying next and do some pre-learning before a lesson so I can arrive with questions.

20 When I hit an obstacle in my understanding, I tend to go looking for solutions, like watching a video, looking it up or asking a teacher.

How might a list like this be useful? You could use the suggestion from the previous chapter and try a never/sometimes/always analysis, but there are other ways forward too. Here's another way in which a list like this might change student behaviour.

Place students in comfort, stretch and challenge zones

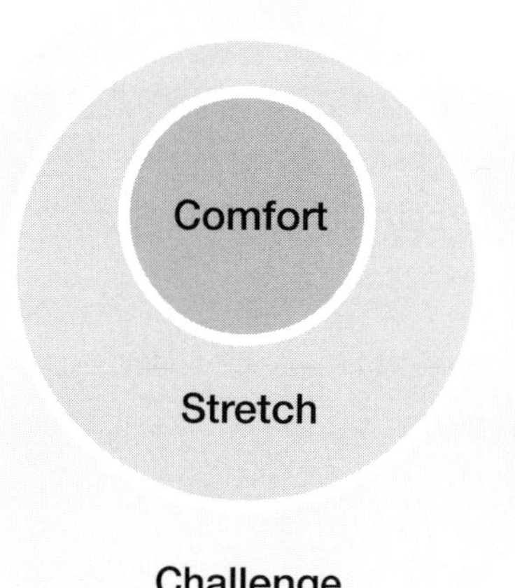

Ask your students to consider which activities belong in their *comfort* zone. These are the ones they'd feel fine taking on straight away and wouldn't involve a huge amount of discomfort.

Next, they should list the activities that belong in their *stretch* zone. These are the ones they could do with a few changes to their routine, even though they might feel a little uncomfortable or unusual to begin with. We sometimes find these are activities the students used to do but haven't for a long time, or they're ones they've seen others do but never tried themselves.

Then we ask students to complete their *challenge* zone. These are behaviours that seem a little scary when they consider them – the ones they'd feel uncomfortable doing and that might take a bit of courageous planning.

Once they have their three lists, we can challenge students to try some behaviours from their stretch zone that they don't do often or, when they're feeling confident, to try some from the challenge zone. We often advise that they work on these new behaviours for a week or two, and stick with them until they begin to feel comfortable.

9. Effort Activity: Proactive versus Reactive

There are two types of work that you do on any course.

Reactive work is completed in response to instruction. This includes classwork, where, during a lesson, a teacher asks you to discuss something in pairs, or complete a particular task, or asks you a question. Reactive work also includes homework; although you do it in your own time, you're doing a task chosen by someone else with a deadline they've set.

Then there's *proactive* work. This is the work you set yourself. No one has asked you to tidy your notes, rewrite a topic summary or create some flash cards – you've done it because you know it will help.

We've interviewed thousands of students and asked them about their levels of reactive versus proactive effort. Here's what we've found.

Entirely reactive	**Mostly reactive but proactive on rare occasions**	**A balance of reactivity and proactivity**	**Some reactivity but mostly proactive**
These students only complete work if they're told to do so. They've often never set themselves any work – even in the run-up to exams, they go to extra classes and react to the instructions they get there.	These students complete almost all their work because they're told to do so. Now and again, if there's a crisis, they'll spend a small amount of time proactively revising for a test or tracking down some missing notes.	These students are close to matching their reactive work with proactive work. They're regularly setting themselves work – rereading and tidying notes, asking questions, reading textbooks and submitting redone essays.	These students get their reactive study out of the way quickly, completing it to a high standard so they can get on with more proactive work. They enjoy the proactive work, exploring topics in detail and challenging themselves.

Outcomes:	Outcomes:	Outcomes:	Outcomes:
These students almost always get the lowest grades in the year group.	These learners find themselves towards the bottom of most groups but have the potential to climb up.	These students tend to be in the middle or towards the top of most of their classes.	These students are almost always at the top of their classes, and often end up getting places at the best universities.

What Does This Mean for You?

A good way to ensure much better grades is to shift your focus towards proactive study. This isn't easy if you've never done it before. Below are some suggestions for how you might begin – twenty-one possible pieces of work you could set yourself.

We've split them into three groups. The *easy tasks* – the first seven – just consolidate your classroom learning. Try these if you've never worked proactively before. The *medium tasks* extend you beyond the classroom work and really boost your learning. Try these if you're feeling confident. The last seven, *the challenges*, are great if you're on top of everything and really exploring beyond the syllabus.

Easy:

1 Tidying and reorganising your notes.

2 Borrowing someone's notes.

3 Reviewing your feedback to look for patterns.

4 Handing a piece of homework in early and asking for advice on how to improve it before deadline day.

5 Completing a one-hour reread and reorganise of notes on any topic.

6 Attending a support class or revision session.

7 Summarising a topic in a single page of notes and diagrams.

Medium:

8 Seeking a book/study guide recommendation from a teacher.

9 Handing in a redone piece of work.

10 Sending five emails asking for support, help, advice or an opportunity.

11 Asking five complex questions of a teacher and noting down the answers.

12 Listening to a podcast related to a topic you've studied.

13 Watching a video summary of a topic and making fresh notes as you go.

14 Seeking out three short exam questions related to a topic and completing them under timed conditions.

Challenges:

15 Beginning a personal project to explore a topic studied at a level above yours.

16 Contacting employers or employees to ask questions.

17 Volunteering to teach someone else the topics you know inside out.

18 Seeking out a reading list for a subject at a higher level than yours.

19 Entering a competition or challenge.

20 Organising a study visit to an employer or place of study.

21 Interviewing a student working at a higher level than you and summarising their advice in notes.

Getting Started and Building Up

Starting out. In the early stages of learning to be proactive, try to complete one or two proactive tasks a week, spending about half an hour on each. Choose the 'easy' ones.

Aiming for a balance. Once you're more confident, you can up your proactive hours, closing the gap between your reactive and proactive study until they're balanced. You might be able to do this by completing loads of the easy tasks above, but the likelihood is you'll be doing some 'medium' ones too. You'll begin to see your grades improve – your teachers might even express some surprise at how well you're doing!

Hitting your stride. Once you're close to a balance of reactive and proactive, try introducing a few of the tasks labelled 'challenges' into your working week. By this time, you'll be regularly performing well in tests and exams and should feel much more optimistic and confident!

10. Effort Activity: The Peloton

In cycling, the word peloton is used to describe a group of cyclists who ride close together. They do this to preserve energy; riding alongside others reduces the drag you get from the air, so there's less wind resistance and it's easier to speed along. Apparently, if you're cycling in the middle of a peloton, surrounded by other riders, you're experiencing just 10% of the drag you would if you were out on your own at the front.

In a race situation, pelotons don't last forever. There's a stage of the race when they're useful, but if everyone stuck in the peloton all the time, the pack would cross the line together. Instead, one rider eventually decides to go for it. They push hard, leave the peloton and race for the finish. Other riders follow. The peloton becomes a stretched out line of cyclists all pedalling for the win.

We've taught hundreds of classes over the last twenty years, and it's interesting to see pelotons in action in classroom situations. Some students – just a few to begin with – are out in front and working hard. Some are at the back, doing virtually no work at all and falling further and further behind. But most stick in the peloton, working hard enough to get by. Then, as the exams approach, everything changes.

Where Are You?

For each of your subjects, you've already chosen where to be in the pack of riders. In some subjects you might be the cyclist out in front, pedalling hard. These might be subjects you love, with teachers you get on well with or topics that interest you. In others, you might be out at the back. In some, you'll be in the peloton.

Consider your current position in each of your subjects. Think carefully. Sometimes it's tempting to put yourself at the back because you're feeling bad, but to do this accurately you have to consider yourself honestly against the other riders.

» Who's out in front? How do you know? What are they doing differently?

» Who's average, sticking in the peloton, preserving their energy and biding their time? How do you know? What are their typical behaviours?

» Who's currently towards the back, and how do you know?

Once you've thought about this you can more accurately consider your position in the pack and label it below.

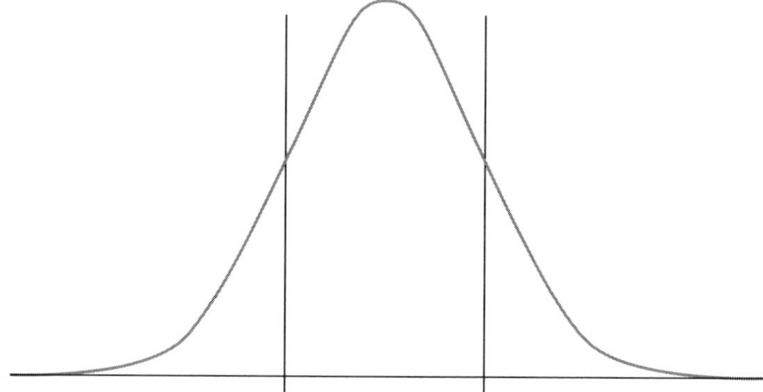

Some riders win the race by being out at the front right from the start. Some win by sticking towards the front of the peloton and timing their charge for the finish perfectly. Some surprise everyone by speeding ahead from out of nowhere. There are lots of ways to do it.

» What would you need to do to move up the pack?

» Choose one, two or three actions that might push you further forward and make a note of them.

» Now schedule one of them – and get it done.

11. Effort Activity: Becoming Indistractable

Lecturer and consultant Nir Eyal has written a book, *Indistractable* (2019), in which he explores why it is we find our lives controlled by tech giants thousands of miles away, even when we have something important to do right in front of us. Often, our time slips away in a haze of checking social media, sending text messages and looking at cat videos – and, before we know it, we've spent two hours half concentrating on something we could have finished in thirty minutes if we'd only been fully focused.

We've found that for many students, the key to increasing levels of effort is decreasing levels of distraction. Eyal suggests something we've found really useful. He argues we should recognise that discomfort (i.e. something that feels hard or boring) precedes distraction, so we need to be ready for it. We shouldn't sit down to do an hour's hard work without first admitting, 'I'm going to feel uncomfortable and then I'll look for distractions. I need to be ready.'

Once we've admitted this to ourselves, we can anticipate distraction.

Where might it come from? Eyal maintains that we need to keep our eyes on two places: the external triggers in the environment around us and the internal triggers we feel inside ourselves. Here are some examples:

External triggers	**Internal triggers**
» Phone alerts for text messages, updates, likes, new videos, etc. » The behaviour of those around you – people coming to chat or ask questions » TV in the background » Radio stations, music	» Hunger » Thirst » Loneliness » Boredom » Insecurity » Negative self-talk ('What's the point? Why do I even have to do it? This task is stupid!')

External triggers	Internal triggers
Others?	Others?
....	....
....	....
....	....
....	....
....	....
....	....
A possible solution:	**A possible solution:**
Use indistractable spaces	Use indistractable routines

Indistractable Spaces

One of the solutions to our external triggers is to design 'indistractable spaces'. These are spaces that are quiet and calm, that promote concentration and feature none of the devices or people we associate with distraction.

Design or discover an indistractable space. What might it look like? What might it contain? Where might it be? When might it be at its best for you?

Many of the most successful students we've worked with have 'airplane mode' on their phone as a feature of their indistractable space.

Indistractable Routines

Eyal suggests that most internal triggers are sudden urges to do something else, and that these urges typically pass within ten minutes. Indistractable routines help with this.

Design a study period (with breaks) that will maximise your chances of concentrating for the full period. How long would it be, and how would the breaks work? (Twenty minutes of work with a five-minute break? Thirty minutes on, then fifteen minutes off?) Think about chunking the session so you move through phases. (Could you do fifteen minutes of note-taking, then a fifteen-minute exam question? Or twenty minutes of preparation for a ten-minute test?) Finally, consider the rewards that might come with successful completion. (A ten-minute check of social media? A walk and a chat? A cup of coffee?)

Combining the Two

Once you've got your indistractable space and your indistractable routine, put the two together. Schedule a study session for some time in the next day or two and try it out. You never know – it might mean you get way more done in less time!

12. Effort Activity: Disruption Cost and Deep Work

Gloria Mark, a professor of informatics at the University of California, Irvine is particularly interested in examining what she calls 'disruption cost' – the amount of time or energy we lose because of interruptions to our work (Mark et al., 2008).

The observation she makes is this: if you're disrupted during work, you lose the number of seconds the disruption took – maybe thirty seconds if someone stops to say hello and exchange a few words – but you lose something else too.

In one experiment Mark ran, she gave university students an email inbox to work through. Then she had actors interrupt them as they tried to work. One group of students had no interruptions, while other groups had varying types of disruption. Then she timed how long it took the students to complete their inbox task.

Here's what she found: all the students completed the task in roughly the same amount of time – just over twenty minutes.

Hang on, you might be thinking, doesn't that disprove Mark's ideas about disruption cost? Well, here's what she did next. She measured the levels of certain feelings in the participants: 'stress', 'frustration', 'time pressure', 'workload' and tiredness because of task-directed 'effort'. And she discovered that the students who had been interrupted felt significantly higher levels of all of these. They got the task done in the same time because they powered through, but 'people in the interrupted conditions experienced a higher workload, more stress, higher frustration, more time pressure, and effort' (Mark et al., 2008, p. 4).

Avoiding Distraction Cost – Introducing Deep Work

One way you can avoid all the bad things associated with disruption – all the frustration and pressure – is to design study sessions differently. Rather than interrupt yourself by switching topics or stressing yourself out by working in places where you'll get sidetracked or disrupted, you can organise your study so you work deeply and with concentrated effort on the same thing for a period of time.

In his book *Deep Work*, the academic Cal Newport (2016) argues that tricky, demanding tasks require us to work deeply. By 'deep work' he means work that is challenging; that requires extended periods of effortful concentration and hard thinking. When we sequence periods of deep work, we minimise distraction cost and lower our levels of stress and frustration – and, as a result, we get more done.

Begin by making a list of possible deep work tasks. Choose tasks that are going to require high levels of effort – tasks you'd love to get done without distraction or stress.

1 ....

2 ....

3 ....

4 ....

5 ....

Now, timetable a deep work study session and attach a tricky task to it. The table below might help you to plan it out.

<table>
<tr><td colspan="3">Deep work topic:</td></tr>
<tr><td colspan="3">What exactly do I need to get done? (The more detail here, the better.)</td></tr>
<tr><td>Date:</td><td>Start time:</td><td>End time:</td></tr>
<tr><td colspan="3">Location(s): (Choose somewhere where you'll minimise distraction cost. Some students we work with like changing location midway through their session as the movement gives them energy and focus.)</td></tr>
<tr><td colspan="3">Reward: (Do something good to celebrate!)</td></tr>
</table>

You could do a deep work session every week and begin a high-effort habit. Soon, you'll find you can get more done – your feelings of control will go up and you'll feel lower levels of stress and pressure. That can only be a good thing.

13. Effort Activity: Questify

Questify is a great tool to use if you've got a task ahead of you that you're dreading. We all have pieces of work like this – ones that feel so horrible, such a terrible slog, that we just can't summon the effort and we do anything to put them off.

If that's the case with a task you've got on your plate, try turning it into a quest.

Questify the whole experience. Make it epic. Set aside a whole afternoon to tackle it; take snacks with you, tell everybody you're off to battle the dreaded job in hand and then put your phone on airplane mode. On the day, keep going until, exhausted, you finally defeat it.

We've seen it work for many students in the past because they've included some important elements in their quest. There are five common characteristics – don't skip them! They're the elements that make the quest feel real, and they seriously increase your chances of success.

1 **Location.** The best quests take you away from familiar spaces. Don't choose your usual study spots and certainly don't stay at home – there are way too many temptations for you there. Quests should require you to travel, taking you away from your usual habits and routines. Consider a library you don't go to often, a coffee shop on the other side of town, a hotel lobby you can reach by a short ride on public transport, your gran's house, or go into work with a parent and borrow a corner of their workspace. All these options make the quest feel real.

2 **Food and drink.** You're not going to be hijacked by hunger. Pack a couple of sandwiches or take two or three snacks that you'll enjoy breaking open when things get tough. You'll need plenty of water too.

3 **Publicity.** One of the ways you'll find that quests motivate you is by putting you *on the hook*. If you tell your parents, peers of friends that you're off to slay a terrible task and by the evening it will all be done, you're going to feel a fool if you end up bailing out. Force yourself to do it by telling others about your plan.

4 **Radio silence.** For the duration of the epic battle, you need to make sure you have no contact with the outside world. You'll need complete concentration during the quest, so switch off Wi-Fi or alerts. The only call you'll make or take will be from your parents to sort out lifts or other issues. Make sure you go totally dark apart from this one important

exception: find and download a study playlist – search ‘music for concentration’ and you’ll discover loads of them – and make sure that’s the only thing you listen to until you’ve slayed the beast.

5 **Celebration.** Finally, all great quests finish with the hero (that’s you!) returning from afar having defeated the dreadful monster. Then there’s a big party in the square and you’re lifted up onto the shoulders of the townsfolk while a band plays celebratory music. OK, you might not be able to get that to happen, but make sure you’ve lined up something great to enjoy when you’re done!

And that’s it – the five rules to successful questing. Good luck out there, adventurer …

14. Effort Activity: Activating and Sustaining

We hear a lot of talk about motivation, but have you ever looked at a definition? We hadn't thought about the concept properly until we did this some years ago. We thought we knew what it meant, but in fact we had only a simplistic understanding of the word. Maybe you're the same.

Motivation is the *ability to initiate and sustain goal-oriented effort*. *Initiate* means to begin; sometimes we need motivational tactics just to get us started. *Sustain* means to continue once we've started; sometimes we need motivational tactics to keep us at it.

So, what techniques might we use to motivate ourselves to put effort into our studies? And should we be using the same techniques to initiate as we do to sustain?

Have a look at the following twenty techniques and choose which ones you might use to initiate effort (to get you started on something) and sustain effort (to keep going even when things are tough).

1 Scaring yourself by imagining failing everything.

2 Begging for a £20 cash payment for every good grade you get.

3 Devising a punishment for not doing work.

4 Telling yourself, 'I'll just do twenty minutes, then I'll stop.'

5 Developing a clear sense of why grades are important and the freedom they can give you.

6 Listing the grades you want and then telling other people that's what you're aiming for.

7 Looking in the mirror and shouting, 'Come on! You can do this! Let's go!'

8 Scheduling a small reward after every hour of work.

9 Comparing yourself to others who are working harder and imagining that they're revising right now and you aren't.

10 Deactivating all your favourite apps on your phone and choosing a date when you're going to reactivate them.

11 Looking at your worst grade and feedback to make yourself feel so bad you do some work.

12 Making a list of topics and ticking them off one by one as you revise them.

13 Visualising the consequences of success.

14 Making a list of all the family and friends who would be really proud of you if you worked hard and did your best.

15 Offering to revise something so you can teach it to someone else.

16 Putting an inspirational quote over your desk or using it as your phone wallpaper.

17 Keeping a calendar and crossing off each day if you've done some work that day.

18 Having a start time that you stick to every single day with an alarm that goes off on your phone at that time.

19 Speaking out loud to yourself, going through a prepared speech that starts, 'I'm doing this because …' or 'I'm working hard *now* because in the future …'

20 Arranging to meet someone else so you can test each other once you've covered a topic.

We're not making any judgements about any of these possible techniques – they might all work for you in certain situations. Consider these questions: are techniques for initiating effort the same as techniques for sustaining effort? What happens to the person who only has motivational techniques for initiating effort? What happens if the only techniques you have are for sustaining effort?

Make a list of your best tactics for initiation and your best for sustaining effort. Ask other people what their tactics are and steal the best to add to your list. Now print off your list and display it prominently.

The next time you're in a rut, look back at your list and pick a technique that you think will most likely work!

15. Effort Activity: The Clarity Countdown

Students have to deal with hundreds if not thousands of pieces of information each week. Every teacher is convinced that their course is the most important, and they're all throwing out new content every day – new ideas, new topics, new vocabulary ... It can be exhausting just keeping up.

But it can get way worse if we fall behind. New ideas arrive and we still haven't figured out the old ones; we start new topics but we don't fully understand the bits we're supposed to have finished. Over time, these tricky, half-understood topics can build up and build up – and pretty soon there's huge amounts of stuff we haven't got our heads around. It can feel overwhelming and stressful.

If this describes you, the following activity could be really helpful. It's like a safety system to prevent you from falling behind.

Here's how it works. Begin by attending a class and staying alert. Listen carefully to the content, engage with the topic and as soon as something crops up that you don't understand, imagine that a countdown clock starts ticking.

You have until the end of the day to get clarity on this confusing point. You cannot let this confusion wait – it'll only get worse with time. You must sort it out *on the day*. Don't worry, though: you have five chances to get clarity while your clock is ticking. We've organised them from immediate to delayed.

Immediate ⟵⟶ Delayed

Chance 1	**Chance 2**	**Chance 3**	**Chance 4**	**Chance 5**
Raise your hand and ask the teacher right then and there.	Wait until the end of class and ask the teacher.	Ask another class member for a quick one-minute recap.	Go to see the teacher at lunchtime or at the end of the day and ask.	Research the issue yourself at home using a textbook or online resource.
This gets the problem solved quickest and lowers your stress levels. But, it can be embarrassing to use over and over. However, if in doubt, go for it.	This is also a quick-solve and avoids the issue of slowing down the whole class. But, sometimes teachers are in a rush and don't have time. However, most will make a few minutes for you, so it's worth it.	This is a speedy solution, too, and can often give you quick clarity. But, sometimes your peers are also confused and can't help. However, if you pick the right student, you can often get the answer you need.	This is a delayed response, so by the time you get there, you may not be able to fully express your confusion. But, you often get a few minutes more of your teacher's attention and get the answer you need.	This is the most delayed of responses, and you're left on your own trying to figure out the tricky topic. But, you can take your time, and spend twenty minutes or half an hour to be sure you've really got it.

The alternative is to let confusing information go and never resolve it. We've seen this happen with plenty of students over the years, and it's not a nice situation to be in. These poor folks often end up stressed, baffled and dreading tests and exams.

By trying a clarity countdown, you might put yourself under a little more pressure on the day, but you ensure that problems don't build up. Why not try:

» **Using a clarity countdown for a particular subject.** Commit to doing this in your maths class or a tricky run of lessons in biology or English. Reserve a small amount of time for clarity countdown work at the end of each day. Keep it up until you feel you're through the challenging section of the course.

» **Using a clarity countdown for all subjects but for a short period of time.** This works particularly well in the run-up to tests, mock exams or even the real thing. It can be an intense week or fortnight, but you end it knowing you're absolutely on top of everything. And your future self will thank you for it!

16. Effort Activity: Red Flag Rescue Plans

It can feel really good to begin a new habit.

You might have planned to put more effort into your work – and for a week or so, it's been working. You've paid attention in class, taken part in discussions and offered a few answers to open questions. You might even have completed a piece of work to twice your normal standard and handed it in early. Things have been going great! Except … now you're feeling your motivation fade. You can sense yourself slipping back into old patterns.

What can we do when we feel our positive start ebbing away? That's when red flag rescue plans come in. Creating one of these now is a great way of preventing slips in the future. It's a simple three-part plan which helps you to keep an eye on yourself.

When a good habit fades, it doesn't collapse in one disastrous afternoon; it falls apart in two stages.

Stage 1: Small Slips and Excuses

Slips feel insignificant to start with. They happen now and again, and we often find ourselves excusing them. It's no big deal. And that's true – if you spot them and adjust. Everyone's slips are different, but look out for things like:

» You let one lesson go by and realise you just weren't paying attention.

» You realise your work has got scrappy and you haven't engaged in classroom activities.

» You notice you've rushed off a homework in ten minutes; deep down you know it's poor.

» Your gaming and TV time has gone up a lot over a few days – usually a sign that you're avoiding something.

Stage 2: Red Flags

This is where the fade gets more serious. It's when several slips combine over a few days or a week. Things begin to feel like they're falling apart. Look out for issues like:

» You notice three lessons have gone by and you've switched off in all of them and missed some crucial stuff.

» A topic seems to be hard, but for days now you've just ignored it.

» You've skipped study sessions and haven't gone back to check over class notes for almost a week.

» You're using social media, games, videos and other distractions much more regularly.

It's your job to put a rescue plan in place at this point. As soon as a red flag goes up, you need to take evasive action to get back on track.

The Rescue Plan

Everyone's rescue plan will be different; the more varied, the better. Think of all the things you could do if you notice red flags going up. It could be options such as:

» Stay behind after school for a couple of nights, go to the library and put in some rescue work.

» Speak to a teacher, admit you're struggling and ask for a recap of a tricky topic.

» Borrow a friend's notes and go through them.

» Ask a class member to talk you through a difficult section or attend a lunchtime catch-up.

By writing these down now, you're strengthening your commitment to them. Students with clear red flags and well-organised rescue plans have two main advantages over everyone else:

1 They've got a list of red flag indicators to watch out for – and these make it much more likely that they spot when a good habit is fading.

2 They have a list of actions to complete as a ready-made solution to a red flag, so they're much quicker at problem-solving.

Use the space below to list what your behaviours look like at each stage, and then make some notes on a possible rescue plan.

Small slips and excuses	Red flags
When a good habit wobbles slightly, I'll know because I tend to do the following:	When a good habit gets into serious trouble and starts to collapse, I'll know because I'll be doing the following:

A red flag rescue plan
When I see red flag behaviours start to happen, I'll take the following action:

Many of us rely on circumstantial reminders or waking-up-in-a-cold-sweat moments to dictate the priority of our tasks.

3. Systems

Systems: the organisational strategies students use to manage their time and resources.

What Do We See When Systems Are Low?

Our project management skills, as well as our time management and resource management skills, are plastic; like any other element of the VESPA model we can improve them with practice. Low-systems students aren't destined for permanently chaotic, high-stress lives. We can demonstrate and model numerous simple tools that they can experiment with and, gradually, we'll see their levels of intentionality and control develop.

When we're working with low-systems students, we'll see proxies in their behaviour that might include some or all of the following. Students' books, files or folders may look disorganised. Resources may be lost or missing. They may have no systems for storing resources at home, which might result in students carrying around everything they've ever been given bursting in a schoolbag or having nothing with them (sometimes not even a pen!). They might have developed a reliance on external reminders to regulate their behaviour – texts, emails or alerts from online systems that tell them when deadlines are approaching. Most of them have never captured everything they have to do in one place, and so their minds are a whirlwind of competing and half-recalled priorities that surface regularly – even at night, when low-systems students are kept awake by suddenly remembered crises. They are sometimes operating without timetables, following their peers around campus and hoping they end up in the right place. Deadlines are missed and all-nighters are pulled. They might have a huge range of progress grades across their courses, from high to very low, because when they intentionally set aside time to achieve something, their tendency is to focus on projects or courses that are going well. They often have only a vague awareness of how a course might be structured or organised, not really knowing where the edges are, and, as a result, may feel frazzled and overwhelmed ('Where does this course end?').

In the minds of low-systems students, these crises expand until they feel huge and impossible. We often speak to these students in January and February when they come to tell us they're quitting – it's all become too much.

It's a very uncomfortable and anxiety-inducing way to live. Luckily, these skills can be taught – and we can help.

Research Spotlight: What the Evidence Indicates

Sean Humpherys and Ibrahim Lazrig ran an interesting study in 2021 at West Texas A&M University, designed to support undergraduates on computing and IT courses with their time management. Not only did they teach time management skills to the 210 students involved in the intervention (a control group were tested but given no support with time management), but they also went on to measure a range of academic outcomes to see if improved time management positively affected performance.

What kinds of things were covered in their time management classes? They were short and sharp fifteen-minute sessions with titles like, 'First Things First', 'Be Proactive' and the Covey-inspired 'Begin with the End in Mind'. Students had to spend class time pre-planning their study weeks in response to specific prompts: 'When will you study next week? Specifically, what days and what times? This is a promise you make to yourself, not to the professor' (Humpherys and Lazrig, 2021, p. 47). They had to list upcoming hand-in dates for assignments and then plan backwards from those dates.

So, what happened? Whereas 5.5% of the control group missed assignment deadlines, that figure dropped to 2.5% for the students given time management support. Interestingly, despite no additional subject-specific instruction, resources or teaching, there were differences in the final grades achieved in the two groups. The control group's final grade was an impressive 92.1%, but the time management group's performance was even better at 94.9% – a statistically significant improvement.

Finally, in terms of qualitative self-reporting, there were additional benefits. Over 85% of students involved described the intervention as 'very helpful'. Some reported that 'the time management skills had an overflow effect that positively impacted their work and life time management', while others reported 'decreased stress consistent with past studies on time management' (Humpherys and Lazrig, 2021, p. 50).

Of course, time management is only one element of systems. Turning our attention to the organisation of resources, there are a range of fantastic studies that examine the link between recording and organising material effectively through note-taking and academic outcomes. Let's look at just one of the many out there.

In Joseph Boyle and Gina Forchelli's (2014) study of ninety high school students, the participants were split according to their levels of achievement – high achievers were getting A grades and average achievers were getting Cs. They were all given a nineteen-minute video lecture about, randomly enough, electric rockets, during which they took notes to record and organise the key ideas and concepts discussed. They then took a comprehension test.

The researchers looked at a range of factors when examining the data: how many words the students had written, whether they had captured and organised what they called 'cued lecture points' (i.e. information preceded by a cue like, 'It's important to remember that …'), whether they'd captured key vocabulary and, of course, what they got on the comprehension test.

There were huge differences in the number of points of information the students collected and organised. High-achieving students wrote 130 words to the average achievers' 86, they were recording 52% of the cued lecture points compared to the average achievers' 27% and collecting 71% of the key vocabulary compared to average achievers' 46%. Ultimately, high achievers scored an average of 75% on the comprehension test to the average achievers' 46%. Correlation is not causation, but the differences are significant, powerful and worthy of further examination.

Other studies emphasise the importance of returning to notes to reorganise and extend them. Kenneth Kiewra, professor of educational psychology at the University of Nebraska-Lincoln, is regularly mentioned or referenced when discussing note-taking, and with good reason. His work in the field is impressive, particularly his focus on the power of returning to notes to reconfigure them, strengthening their organisational structure and drawing out fresh connections between concepts.

In one study, he split students into different groups before they attended a twenty-minute lesson. He restricted each group to a certain note-taking practice before testing their recall at the end. The group who took their own notes, then reviewed them before the test, scored 51%. But those who took their own notes and reviewed them alongside a complete set of notes provided to them scored 71% (Kiewra, 1985) – compelling evidence to support revisiting and restructuring notes alongside a textbook or study guide.

So, what does all this mean for us?

When We're Working with Students ...

Although we wish it were as simple as urging learners to 'get yourself organised', that isn't going to work. Post-COVID-19 learning cohorts have grown up with the idea that resources will be centrally organised on Teams or Google Classroom, and that teachers will give them regular reminders to ensure they meet all deadlines. That kind of micromanagement, where the locus of control lies firmly with the staff, can suffocate the development of the characteristics we want to nurture in students, and instead create learners who expect – and, indeed, wholly rely on – reminders and intervention orchestrated and delivered by the school or college.

Alternatively, here are some of the principles and approaches we've found useful.

1. Complete capture

Very few low-systems students have ever reached the point at which every task, responsibility and job they have to do are written down in one place. Many rely on circumstantial reminders or waking-up-in-a-cold-sweat moments to dictate the priority of their tasks. When we do a complete capture session, it might take thirty minutes of students soul-searching and head-scratching. But, at the end, once they've got absolutely everything written down, we often see their posture change. They walk taller and smile a little more; they're relieved. They don't need to use their brains for remembering tasks any more. They can use them for learning new things.

2. Task boards or to-do lists?

On the surface, task boards and to-do lists might look so similar as to be virtually interchangeable, but we've not found this to be the case. A task board allows for prioritisation almost as the list is being generated; Pending, Doing, Done (Activity 19) or The Energy Line (Activity 17 in *The A Level Mindset*) allow students to make instant decisions about priorities that they can subsequently adjust, whereas a to-do list requires laborious copying out or confusing arrays of scribbled-out numbers.

A reminder: if you're modelling these tools with students, they take a photograph of the finished board and you keep the hard copy. In that way, you can flourish the hard copies a week after the initial session, holding them to account the next time round.

3. A weekly focus on the near future

A small amount of time spent regularly looking ahead with students reduces the fires you'll be fighting later on. If you're a classroom teacher or tutor, consider making a ritual of a 'heads-up session' each Friday, for example. Ten minutes will often do it. 'Let's use our collective memory to remind ourselves what's happening next week. What deadlines have we got coming up? What events are going on? Which teachers are going to be mad if we miss something? What do we need to pack in our bags? Work together to draw up a list of everything you can think of, and then we'll go through it all together.' You might want to scribble this list up on the board and model the process of recording and prioritising as you do so. You could finish with, 'What promises are we going to make to ourselves for next week? What's our weekend looking like as a result?'

4. Files, folders and books

Giving students pockets of time in which to catch up on their resource organisation is critical. A small part of you will feel indignant – 'Why don't they do this on their own time, not mine?' – but remember the power of collective efficacy. Students will do it – and, indeed, enjoy doing it – because everyone else is working away at it as well. They'll see each other tidying their books and folders. They'll watch in awe as a high-systems student double-checks their immaculate handouts and wonder if they could be more like that. They'll borrow glue sticks and reflect on their learning as they neaten inserts and investigate mysterious printouts they'd forgotten all about. They'll realise they've got missing resources and strike deals for replacements, add jobs to their task boards or set reminders on their phones. And, at the end of the session, they'll be feeling a whole lot better.

5. Check and reward progress

Checking and rewarding progress has become a central plank of our work with students. Waiting until students have achieved an outcome before handing out praise can be counterproductive; the goal seems too distant and those who fall behind give up trying. Being clear that you're going to reward process really helps:

> **In the fortnight before half term, I'll be looking for students who've made real progress towards neat and tidy learning resources. So, what we're going to do is check in with where we are now and establish a starting point. Then I'll give you some structured time to tackle it. Then I'm checking again on [insert date]. Whoever has made significant steps forward is getting a reward. I'm looking for progress, not perfection.**

Models are very useful – what exactly does a good set of notes look like? Gather examples of your best students recording and restructuring learning so others can see the standard they're aiming at.

Twenty High-Systems Behaviours

Whenever we're working with high-systems learners, we grill them for ideas, drawing out exactly what it is they're doing to fit everything in and hit their deadlines. We're seeking evidence that they can organise resources, make sense of their myriad learning materials and summarise information in a helpful way so they can offer practical, replicable tactics to others.

Here are the most commonly discussed behaviours we see when we're interviewing high-systems students:

1 I can break down what I need to achieve into small steps, and often do things in more than one sitting rather than all at once.

2 I can summarise and reshape information so that it feels like mine. I might rewrite it or use a table, chart, graph or mind-map.

3 I file my notes in the right place at the end of each day and regularly check they're tidy and accessible.

4 I have an organised workspace at home and in school to study with everything in its place so I can find it quickly.

5 I keep my books and folders in one place in my room/home so I don't lose them.

6 I know what has been covered on my course so far, and ensure it's all there by checking my books against study websites, textbooks or knowledge organisers.

7 I look ahead to next week, checking what needs to be done, so that even when lots of deadlines come at once, I work out how to finish and submit everything.

8 I make mini lists of tasks I have to do at the start of particular periods – like on a Monday or over a weekend – and think about how to prioritise them.

9 I might set reminders for myself – alarms on my phone – or leave notes for myself so I don't forget things.

10 I often list the things I have to do and figure out which order I need to do them in to make the best use of my time.

11 I often start homework four or five days before it's due in and do a bit each night, fitting it around clubs, hobbies, fitness and other activities.

12 I organise my work visually, maybe using colourful stationery or reminders, so I know how the course works.

13 I pack my bag for the next day the night before.

14 I review my notes to ensure they are organised in a beneficial order for revision, sticking in handouts, making a contents page or adding colourful headings.

15 I sometimes check in with friends or classmates, asking when assignments are due or where they're up to with certain tasks, so I know if I have to speed up or catch up.

16 I sometimes make quick daily lists – 'must finish this', 'have to do this', 'get started on this task', etc.

17 I sometimes plan my week in advance, giving myself plenty of time to work on tasks.

18 I sometimes summarise everything we've learned on one page, a series of flash cards or a knowledge organiser.

19 I spend small periods of time double-checking I've done everything I need to or reviewing the last few days.

20 I work out the best way to present a whole course and reorganise everything so it's clear and helpful for me.

How might a list like this be useful? Well, you could try the approaches we suggested under Vision in Chapter 1 (the never/sometimes/always analysis) or, indeed, for Effort in Chapter 2 (the three concentric circles asking students to put habits in comfort, stretch and challenge zones). But there are other ways forward. Here's another approach you might want to consider.

Make an impact analysis

Ask the students to consider all the behaviours listed above and note down which ones they think would make the best impact on their progress and positivity under three headings: 'low impact', 'medium impact' and 'high impact'. Once they're done, they should make a commitment to choose a behaviour they've rated as among the highest and take it on for a week or two. Make sure you prime them to notice the small differences this one behaviour might make.

17. Systems Activity: The Sunday Night Ritual

In his book, *How to Win at College*, writer and professor Cal Newport has the following piece of advice for students studying A levels and degrees at university: Sunday is the most important day of the week. 'Why?' he writes, 'Because Sunday sets the tone for the week that follows.' He adds: 'If you take control of your Sunday, you take control of your week' (Newport, 2005, pp. 17, 18).

Now, we're not recommending you do tons of work on Sunday but, inspired by Newport's advice, we are suggesting that you set aside thirty minutes on Sundays to complete a sort of pre-working week ritual.

This might sound strange, but stick with us.

Your thirty minutes can be at any time of day that suits you, although we like to do our Sunday checklist at around 6pm before we relax for the evening. Your Sunday night ritual should follow a simple ABCD pattern:

A is for activities. What's coming up this week? Is there a PE lesson that needs certain kit? Is there an afterschool club? Do you need to prepare for a Zoom call? Did you promise you'd lend something to someone? Do you need to reply to an email?

B is for bag. What needs to go in your bag this week? A late homework you need to hand in? A book you borrowed from a teacher that you have to return? Are the basics there? Pencil case, pens, books for the right subjects? Bus pass? ID?

C is for crisis. What's getting out of control at the moment? (It happens to all of us.) Is there anything you can deal with this week to avert a disaster? A conversation you need to have? A promise you have to keep? A subject you're behind on? A teacher you need to hassle for help?

D is for deadlines. When is your homework due this week? Are there any tests coming up? Is anything overdue? Are there any signed notes you need to hand in or issues you need to sort out?

Activities	Bag
Crisis	**Deadlines**

Using the ABCD structure for your Sunday night ritual will help to calm your mind. You can kick back and relax on Sunday evenings, knowing you're ready for the week to come. You can sleep well, too, confident you're on top of things.

Who knows, maybe the whole week will be better because of your Sunday night ritual. Like Cal Newport (2005, p. 17) says, get it right on Sunday and 'you will start your week with momentum behind you'.

18. Systems Activity: Night School

There used to be night schools across the country – regular schools and colleges that taught young students by day but would open their doors and teach adults at night.

Night school classes didn't last long – perhaps sixty or ninety minutes – but the teaching always felt very different to day school. Some differences were obvious: no uniform, of course; no assemblies or tutorials; no one using 'Sir' or 'Miss'. Other differences were more subtle. The students who turned up really wanted to be there. They were keen, asked lots of questions, went over their notes in detail and enjoyed the learning process. There was no sitting slumped in a corner, no whispering or checking phones while the teacher looked away; night school students were organised and focused.

For this activity, consider what a night school would look like if you designed it yourself.

There's one student – you. And there's one teacher – you. You get to decide which days of the week it runs and when the classes start and finish. You decide where night school takes place. You're in charge of the curriculum, so each session is designed by you. Most of all, you're in charge of the culture and behaviour. You get to be focused, engaged and interested; you get to do things that fascinate you or turn dull topics into interesting quizzes and activities.

It's a lot to think about and will take some planning, so grab a pen and scribble down some impressions under the following headings.

1. Activities and resources

What would attending your night school feel like? What kinds of activities would be happening? Night school should be active and interesting. Are there videos to watch, new ways of taking notes, colourful summaries, pictures or displays? Are there big sheets of paper and felt-tip pens? Mini whiteboards and quizzes? Is there sometimes a homework club? A 'hard questions' section of the class? A time when you have to give a mini lecture out loud summarising a topic?

2. Rituals and rewards

What are the traditions that always happen? You're the boss, so you could have a night school where you start the session with a blast of music or have the radio on quietly in the background. You could have biscuits or fancy drinks. You could take a break at a certain point or end each session in a certain way. There could be scoreboards, calendars and charts to record progress.

3. Timetable

When would your night school run? Ninety minutes on Tuesdays and Thursdays? Once a week but for two hours? Straight after school or college in that fallow period between 4pm and 5.30pm? Or does it start later after you've had a chance to recharge, running from 7–8.30pm? How might you break down the time? Three thirty-minute sessions? One full hour, then a short blast of admin?

4. Campus

What does your classroom look like? Are you in a branch of a coffee shop or an ice cream parlour? Do you use a library? Is there a room or space on your school/college campus that acts as your HQ? Or is it your bedroom at home? Wherever it is, can you modify the environment a little to indicate that night school is in session? Organise your desk in a certain way, close some curtains, move the furniture or switch off your phone?

Now that you've got some ideas, run night school for a couple of weeks. Start as soon as possible, get into it and see what it feels like. Plan some simple sessions reviewing notes or recapping day school topics. It won't be long before you're getting ahead on your work. You'll understand things more in class; stress and anxiety will melt away. Your grades might improve, and your teachers might seem surprised and delighted. You might even consider combining schools for a session a week with a friend.

19. Systems Activity: Pending, Doing, Done

In this activity, we suggest organising your entire study life into a simple three-part system. It's one we've seen work in a lot of work-based contexts, where employees use what they sometimes call 'task boards' (big whiteboards split into sections) to create quick, visual summaries of everything on their plate.

This three-part task board should help to get you feeling much less stressed and anxious; it gives you an at-a-glance understanding of everything you need to do and what you're currently up to. It looks like this:

Pending			Doing	Done
Cold	Warm	Hot		

OK, some explanation is needed!

Pending is where you put new tasks and jobs as they arrive. You write each task or job on a sticky note, being clear and specific about what it involves – for example, 'Complete geography work started in class', 'Send email to teacher' or 'Write introduction to English essay'. When you place a job in *pending*, you must decide exactly where to put it – *cold* if it's not urgent, *warm* if it needs doing quickly and *hot* if it's a top priority.

Doing is the stuff you're working on right now. You don't want to be overwhelmed by trying to do half a dozen things at once, so there are only three slots here. Move the jobs that are hottest from the *pending*, column into one of the three boxes. This is where you focus your work every day.

Done is where you put your sticky note when you've finished the task. Why not just bin it? Well, speaking to people who use these systems, we hear a lot of them say how motivating it is to fill up the done section of their task board. They might only clear it every few weeks.

And that's it! Pretty simple, but a fantastic, streamlined way of keeping on top of your work.

Of course, you need to review your task board regularly to make sure things are sitting in the correct columns. *Cold*, *warm* and *hot* will need constant reorganising depending on what's coming up and what your deadlines are, for example. Keep on top of it and it might be a lifesaver!

20. Systems Activity: Boosters and Sappers (aka Energy Makes Time)

Former company boss and leadership coach Mandy Brown makes a good point about time management in her blog post, 'Energy Makes Time' (2023). Many of us, she says, have the feeling that we have too much to do and not enough time to do it. Brown argues that when our levels of energy are low, we often take much longer to do tasks that we might otherwise have completed quickly.

You're feeling sluggish, so the maths homework that should've taken half an hour ends up filling fifty minutes of your evening, or the textbook read-through takes twice as long because you find you're not concentrating, or you want to write up some notes but can't find them and … suddenly, you just can't be bothered any more.

The solution, she suggests, is to sequence tasks better. The phrase she uses is 'energy makes time'. In other words, when we're feeling inspired or boosted, our focus lasts longer, we get more done and seem to have more time.

So, could we organise our work in a way that boosts us instead of sapping us?

Take the tasks you do in a typical day's work and choose whether they boost or sap your energy. It's often easy to do this – there's just a feeling we have. But if you find it hard, consider these ideas:

» **The booster.** If you've just organised and completed an energy-boosting task, you've often got just as much or even more energy after you finish an hour's work. These tasks tend to leave you feeling positive, pleased and excited to do more. (They're not necessarily easier subjects or tasks, by the way!)

» **The sapper.** Working on an energy-sapping task feels the opposite. These tasks might not be hard, but they might leave you feeling flat and drained, as if your energy gauge is low.

OK, have a go at this now. Make a list of tasks you've got coming up, then try to assess how they're going to change your levels of energy by adding a pointer to each dial.

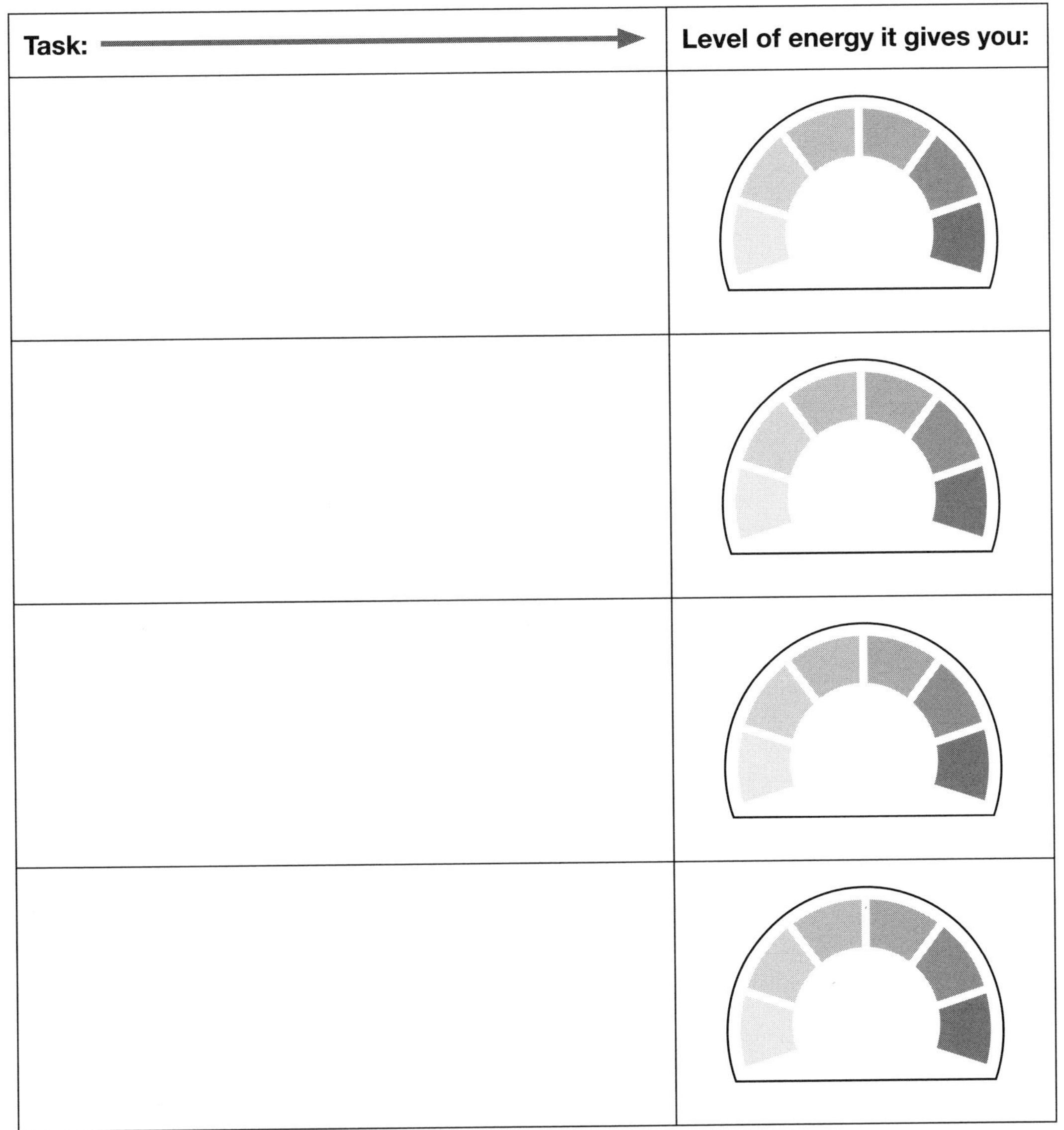

Task: →	Level of energy it gives you:

What themes emerge? What tasks do you thrive doing, and which ones require a bit more grit to complete?

Now organise and sequence a day's work that considers your boosters and sappers. Some of the following advice might help:

» Start your day with a booster. Whatever happens afterwards, you'll have given yourself the energy to push forwards feeling positive.

» Follow a sapper with a booster. If you've got a sapping task, it's often good to have something to look forward to.

» Do two sappers with strict time limits, then give yourself a break. Churning through a couple of tough tasks, and being strict about how much time you're going to spend doing them, deserves a reward. Take a little time off, go for a walk, watch a little TV or play a game. Then begin again with a booster.

» Finish your day with a booster, not a sapper. You don't want that final task of the day extending out as you get more and more exhausted. Aim to finish your day with something that's even a little bit positive.

21. Systems Activity: The Catch-Up Week

Often, we can find ourselves adrift. The term is a few months old and we've fallen behind where we wanted to be; we've let things slip, our systems have collapsed and we know we need to get back on track.

If that describes your situation, what you might need is a catch-up week. A catch-up week is a carefully planned and timetabled week where you work with much more organisation and focus. The aim is to plan like crazy, and then throw yourself into a highly strategic seven days of concentration to recover all that lost ground.

Catch-up weeks need to be planned on paper first, with particular tasks assigned to particular days, even to particular time blocks. You will need to create a checklist of tasks, each of which gets crossed off when it's done.

Planning a week like this can feel daunting, so we've given you a simple place to start. First, collect together all the work you want to catch up on. Some will fill you with dread, other tasks will be fairly straightforward. Then arrange them all somewhere on this continuum:

Least daunting ('I'll quite enjoy this') ←→ **Most daunting** ('I'm dreading this')

Now you can plan your catch-up week. We've suggested a one-big-task-per-day structure, and filled the week with the kind of things you might want to schedule for each day. You could follow our plan if you wanted, but the activity becomes even more effective when you design your own or design one as a study group.

Day 1	Day 2	Day 3	Day 4	Day 5	Day 6	Day 7
Complete: a job you should have done ages ago that really needs finishing *or* a short job that will take thirty minutes and get you started.	*Finish:* a piece of homework ahead of the deadline.	*Complete:* the piece of work you're most dreading *or* explore a possible future career online.	*Complete:* a one-hour reread and rewrite of your notes on any difficult topic.	*Start:* the reading and research for a piece of work you know will be challenging.	*Complete:* a job that's fallen behind schedule *or* a short job that will take thirty minutes or less.	*Finish:* a piece of work to twice the standard you would consider your 'normal' level of effort.

If you can take action on these seven steps as the week goes by, you'll be significantly closer to living that stress-free, pressure-free life we all dream of. And the best thing is, you can celebrate at the end of the week! Take some time off and reward yourself.

So, every time you feel demotivated or overwhelmed, forget the big picture. Instead, make a plan for a super-organised catch-up week. Return to this activity or design one of your own using the advice below to help you.

» Some students plan a week like this at the start of every half term to get them up and running.

» Some students alternate weeks like this – one on, one off.

» Towards exam season or coursework deadlines, we've seen students plan two or three weeks of organised and time-blocked activities to keep them on track.

» The best plans we've seen include rewards, with students scheduling something good to keep them going.

22. Systems Activity: Have To, Ought To, Want To

A lot of our systems activities are about time management. But, what if we have mega-organised time management but we're spending all our precious time efficiently doing the wrong things?

This is where attention management comes in. Attention management tools start by looking at how we're spending our time, and then ask us to consider whether we're doing the right things – the tasks with the biggest impact on our learning and our positivity. Attention management invites us to consider whether we've got a healthy balance of tasks to keep us at our best.

For example: if you worked through a super-organised week of prioritised tasks that were repetitive, boring and (crucially) had little impact on your learning and confidence, you might end up frazzled, exhausted and frustrated.

Instead, you should reconsider the tasks you have to do and plan a week that allows you to complete meaningful work, build for the future and find the space to connect with things that make you happy.

We're calling these three categories have to, ought to and want to. The *have to* zone reduces your anxiety and keeps you on track. The *ought to* zone gives you permission to set aside immediate challenges and build for the future. The *want to* zone keeps you positive, healthy and balanced.

So, what's on your lists? Have a go at filling in the table below.

Have to ... These things feel crucial, and if ignored will keep me awake at night:	**Ought to ...** If I just had time and a little head space, I'd do these helpful jobs/tasks:	**Want to ...** If only I could design my life the way I want it, I'd have more time for:
....	....	....

If we're going to stay positive, we need to design weeks that allow us to move between these three zones. Here are three possible approaches to consider. They each assume you can get ten things done per week, but you might be different so you'll need to plan accordingly.

The *hard-work week* – for churning through tasks and getting things done:

» Seven have tos (choose the most important or the ones with the biggest impact).

» Two ought tos.

» One want to.

The *balanced week* – for staying on top and future planning:

» Five have tos (again, choose the most important or the ones with the biggest impact).

» Three ought tos.

» Two want tos.

The *self-care week* – for refocusing:

» Three have tos (as before, choose the most important or the ones with the biggest impact).

» Four ought tos.

» Three want tos.

Are things in the right category?

Some of the more frazzled and stressed students we speak to miscategorise – they fill the *have to* column with things they don't really have to do. Watch out for this. It's worth considering your *have to* list for a moment. Obviously, homework and other assignments need to be done – there's no room for negotiation here. But are some of the other things really necessary? One student had a huge list of have tos, and when we suggested removing some of them, acknowledged that they weren't crucial but said, 'I'd feel really guilty if I didn't do them.'

It's a very reasonable and understandable response, but saying no to requests is perfectly fine. In the adult world of work, we're constantly negotiating what we have time to do and what work might be best given to someone else. It's not lazy to acknowledge you haven't got time to do something. And you'll have an opportunity to give back once your period of hard work slackens off.

23. Systems Activity: Cornell Notes

You might not think that the way you take notes has any effect on how much you remember or how well you do on a test or exam. However, Professor Kenneth Kiewra at the University of Nebraska-Lincoln has run a range of experiments about note-taking as well as studied many experiments conducted by others (Kiewra et al., 2018).

The key seems to be the work you do *after* you've taken the initial notes. Returning to the notes helps, obviously, but it's not the reading of those notes that necessarily has an impact. It's returning to *develop* the notes through activities like:

» Clarifying material with additional underlining, arrows, subheadings and reminders.

» Adding to the material with 'how' or 'why' questions that work like a test, encouraging you to explain what you're reading.

» Adding to the material with clarifications you've got from textbooks or study guides, expanding the material with deeper additional information.

(Kiewra et al. (2018) show an increase of about 20% in test results if students do this kind of work!)

So, can we take notes in a way that helps this process? We can. This note-taking system is called Cornell Notes (named after an American university.) It looks like this:

Cue	Notes
Summary	

Have a go yourself!

Take your notes as usual in the *notes* section of the page during class.

Use the *cue* column to add keywords, prompts, questions, clarifications, reminders, arrows or additional material. You can do some of this work in class and some of it afterwards when you revisit your learning.

The *summary* section – no surprise here – is for you to summarise your learning. Write two or three sentences of explanation for your future self, so that when you return, you've got a clear sense of what the notes cover.

24. Systems Activity: 1% Planning

Each day, every single one of us has the same number of minutes to spend – 1,440.

In her book, *The Seven Minute Difference* (2006), entrepreneur, coach and writer Allyson Lewis argues that if we spend just 1% of these minutes planning and reflecting, we should be able to spend the other 99% getting on with our work and enjoying our lives. 1% of 1,440 minutes is about fourteen minutes, which Lewis suggests we split into two seven-minute sections.

Inspired by her approach, we've developed our own seven-minute system with a focus on planning study. Here's how our 1% planning works.

Every morning set aside seven quiet minutes

This might seem ridiculously obvious, but it's harder than it looks! You'll quickly realise how much of your day is the noise and activity of conversations, arguments, cafes and canteens, TV, social media, gaming and travel. You'll need to find a space and time when none of that applies. You'll need something to write on (we like using a single flash card for this activity), and you'll need to be totally focused. Once you're ready to go, scribble notes under the following headings. The aim is to have three things you really want to do.

- **What one thing needs *completing* today?** Select one thing you want or need to finish and cross off today, no negotiation. This is your must do.
- **What one thing needs *further work* today?** Choose one thing you need to continue working on today – something you've already started but needs attention.
- **What one thing needs *starting* today?** Select one thing you haven't begun yet but you need to get going on today.
- **Leftovers.** Throw down everything else that's on your mind here.

Completing:	Leftovers:
Further work:	
Starting:	

Then, at the end of the day …

Every evening set aside seven quiet minutes

Again, harder than it looks – but do your best to make sure you've got this small pocket of time to think back over the day and check through what happened. We find these five areas of questioning and reflection really useful:

» How did your day go? Did you get your three things done? What's left over?

» What's tomorrow looking like as a result?

» What's on your longer range radar? (This is a brain dump that should take a couple of minutes – write down anything and everything that you know is coming up on the flash card.)

» In your studies, what do you need to do more of?

» In your studies, what do you need to do less of?

You might want to use the other side of the flash card for this reflection.

And that's it – your day is finished. Tomorrow gets another flash card and a fresh start.

If this system ever feels difficult or time-consuming, remember – it isn't actually that bad. You still get 99% of your time to spend getting on with your day. And just because the 1% is a tiny time period, it doesn't mean it isn't effective. Just these two small pockets of quiet thinking and planning could make a massive difference to your sense of calm, your levels of stress and your feelings of control.

That's the power of 1% planning!

The revision strategies that have the greatest impact feel the most uncomfortable, and slow our sense of progress. And anything that compromises that feeling of fluency may be seen as a threat.

4. Practice

Practice: the type and amount of revision students complete in preparation for tests and exams.

What Do We See When Practice is Low?

First, a reminder that, like any other metacognitive element of study, the way we practise can change as we pay attention to it and then intentionally focus our efforts on developing and improving it. Low-practice students are capable of working differently; it's not beyond their intellectual capabilities. However, it can be a scary prospect.

When high-practice behaviours are missing, we'll see proxies that might include some or all of the following. Low-practice students might conceive of revision as the process of 'reseeing' something, with the semantic emphasis squarely on 'vision'. They might have heard instructions like 'review' your work, and have interpreted this literally, so their personal definition of revision is something like 'passively looking at information for a second time'. As a result, they might double down on rereading, perhaps staring at notes multiple times in the hope that they 'go in'. They almost always focus their attention on collecting, curating and reading notes rather than using their knowledge to solve problems under timed conditions, and so often have narratives that explain their underperformance in tests, such as, 'I know everything really well, but on the day of the test my mind goes blank' or 'I'm going to enrol on courses that require portfolio work because I'm no good at exams.' (When these students tell us they know everything really well, by the way, they invariably don't.) They might feel that recalling notes without being able to see them is unrealistic. Fearing the possibility that information may degrade over time, or be forgotten altogether, they favour cramming it all in at the last minute. They might write on both sides of flash cards and passively reread them, rather than use a question-and-answer structure to test recall and using only one side of the flash card for information so they can cover it up. They might refuse to engage in more challenging revision, saying it doesn't work for them; they avoid the discomfort that comes from operating at the edge of their ability. They might express frustration at their progress or anger that they revise hard but go on to underperform. They often resort to throwing even more time at the problem, staying up late reading notes for even longer, mistakenly thinking that effort is the issue. The idea of revising with someone else or creating a study group might strike them as odd ('What would we do – read in silence together?') because the possibility of two people testing each other feels uncomfortable.

It's a set of behaviours that is entirely understandable. Changing them takes time and patient persistence, but it is possible. The activities in this chapter should give you a place to start, but first let's look at the evidence.

Research Spotlight: What the Evidence Indicates

One of the undoubted urtexts in this area, a starting point at which we all usually begin, is John Dunlosky's 'Improving students' learning with effective learning techniques: promising directions from cognitive and educational psychology' (Dunlosky et al., 2013). Dunlosky and his Kent State University team's meta-analysis of ten learning techniques and their impact on test performance is a significant and important synthesis of the current research on effective practice. We cover the paper in Activity 25 (High and Low Utility), but the headlines, in case you're not familiar with it, are that the highest utility revision techniques (that is, impact on test performance) are practice testing, followed by spaced practice (for an activity around this, check out Activity 31: Spaced Practice in *The GCSE Mindset*). The research may be brilliant, but that doesn't mean it's easy to operationalise. Anyone who's delivered their Dunlosky session to students, then checked in a week later to find the entire cohort continuing to read notes and highlight key terms, will know this. High-utility revision strategies aren't straightforward to adopt immediately because:

» In order to do the work that has the greatest impact – practice tests and spaced practice – students first need a complete set of notes from which to work. That means going through their class notes, resources and handouts to prepare them for revision. It's a task that can take many hours, as well as one that feels safe and comfortable, so it expands to fill all the available time. Thus, we find students who are choosing to make entirely updated mind-maps, incorporating new and recently purchased pastel-hued highlighters, rather than test themselves.

» The revision strategies that have the greatest impact feel the most uncomfortable, and their difficulty slows our sense of progress. It's this sense of progress that students respond to ('I have a lot to learn, so I enjoy it when I feel like I'm blasting through large amounts of material quickly'), and anything that compromises that feeling of fluency can be seen as a threat. You might have heard students tell you they have tried covering up notes and recalling them from memory (see Activity 26: Closed Book Note-Taking,) but it felt hard, slowed them down and didn't work for them, so they're returning to reading and highlighting.

» In the past, students may have been told that revision is 'revisiting and reviewing information in order to embed it'. Students who hear this regularly will naturally choose activities which support that process. Our alternative definition of revision, should it be helpful, is 'improving learning materials through clarification, reconstruction and reorganisation, so they can be readily recalled and used to solve problems under timed conditions'.

So, the challenges we face in frameworking effective revision are real. If it's any consolation, it seems that students tend to discover the power of high-utility revision themselves later in their academic careers. Lerchenfeldt and Nyland's (2016) study of second-year medical students at Oakland University in Michigan confirms this. Students were taught a new section of the course and then set tests on the content. They were asked to report how long they spent revising using eight specific techniques taken from Dunlosky et al. (2013). Although the sample size was small (twenty-one participants), the researchers found that the students (all of them at least two or three years older than the ones we are working with, and all of them with a track record of strong academic results), spent 51% of their time using low-utility revision techniques while compiling and organising their notes. However, by the time they reached the 'pre-exam period', they spent 47% of their time on practice testing – an impressive figure. This shift towards practice testing in the run-up to exams is what we need to encourage earlier.

In terms of the strategies students used and their test outcomes, the findings differ slightly from Dunlosky's. Four revision techniques correlated with underperformance in tests: rereading notes, highlighting/underlining while reading, writing summaries of topics and memorising using mnemonics (three out of four correlate with Dunlosky's findings; his team found stronger evidence for the positive impact of writing summaries but confirmed the negative impacts of the other methods). Two were correlated with stronger performance – practice tests and explaining how complex ideas connect to each other – both of which map reasonably well onto Dunlosky's research, although he finds a higher impact in his study. One significant difference was Lerchenfeldt and Nyland's (2016) findings about 'turning information into images', a revision technique that had a much stronger effect than Dunlosky discovered, particularly in the hours immediately before an exam, possibly they say, because the material can be more easily represented by pictures.

Another study worth our attention is the work of Afton Kirk-Johnson at the University of Pittsburgh (Kirk-Johnson et al., 2019). Kirk-Johnson explores a fascinating component of student revision – how students feel as they revise and how those feelings impact future revision choices. She notes that 'learners cannot accurately assess what they have learned and what study techniques will help them learn'. Instead, they 'must infer what they know and how well they are learning on the basis of various cues … Many learners appear to use *in-the-moment processing fluency* to monitor their learning … So, many learners who encounter difficulty or disfluency in their learning may interpret these struggles as a sign of failure' (Kirk-Johnson et al., 2019, p. 2; our emphasis).

Kirk-Johnson explores how this feeling of disfluency plays out in subsequent study choices. She gave large cohorts (between seventy and eight-nine students) information to learn and then offered them a choice about how to revise it. In one study, the choice given was either to restudy and reread the material or to actively recall the information through testing. Some 69% of students chose the former, based on their assessment of how hard it would be – how much effort they would have to expend – and their likely levels of success. It's an important component of the puzzle; as Kirk-Johnson writes: 'learners infer how well a study strategy contributes … based in part on the experience of mental effort … Strategies experienced as more mentally effortful are interpreted as less effective … and, consequently, not chosen' (Kirk-Johnson et al., 2019, p. 15).

When We're Working with Students …

As the divers and thrivers study we explored in the introduction showed (Beattie et al., 2016), we need to emphasise the importance of regular maintenance beating one-off mega-sessions; reiterate the fact that, when it comes to learning information, consistency beats intensity. Students who are regularly engaged in some sort of practice, snacking rather than bingeing, will be the ones who perform best. An example: spaced practice requires students to revisit half-forgotten topics and relearn them on a regular basis rather than learning them once in a single session of cramming the night before an exam. Only those who practise regularly, little and often over a longer period, can leverage this particular effect.

Other issues that deserve further exploration include the following.

1. Discussing the phases of practice is crucial, with students and parents

Revision or practice is not one amorphous process, but a staged one. First comes the *preparation* phase – the collecting and organising of material. In this phase, we might rewrite our notes, turn them into mind-maps, sequence them on flash cards, read course textbooks, watch tutorials and triple-check we have everything covered. Then comes the *performance* phase when we're turning mere information into knowledge by using it to solve problems under timed conditions. We're practising subject-specific skills, which we repeatedly execute in short bursts or micro-exams – ten, twelve or fifteen minutes spent under exam conditions struggling with a tricky question. And we seek feedback on our performance to improve it – we check our recall, study mark schemes, submit extra work, mark our own work, estimate what grade we might get and check model answers. The performance phase pushes us so that we operate at the edge of our ability. It requires cognitive resources; it's mental combat, so it's threatening to the ego ('What if I discover I'm terrible at this?') and, quite naturally, students do everything they can to avoid it. (For a longer discussion of these three stages – collecting content in the preparation phase, then executing on subject-specific skills and seeking feedback – have a look at our Revision Questionnaire (Activity 25) in *The A Level Mindset*).

2. Urging change won't be enough

Because of the cognitive challenge of high-utility revision, students will need more than a quick assembly with a couple of demonstrations. There's a trade-off with high-utility revision: it requires more cognitive resources in the moment, so it feels as if it's breaking the fluency of progress. As a result, students steer clear. Therefore, we need to share practical modelled examples of new techniques with which learners have time to experiment, and we need to reassure them that, although they will feel harder, they will be more beneficial to their learning.

3. Difficulty is desirable

Many of us may know of the work of Elizabeth and Robert Bjork at the University of California, Los Angeles, in particular their focus on the notion of desirable difficulty. Bjork says it best in this extract from his paper presented at the Integrating Cognitive Science with Innovative Teaching in STEM Disciplines conference at Washington University in 2012: 'learners should break away from the misconception that the most effective ways of learning are those that make learning easy. The experience of having to expend effort, generate errors, or work hard to achieve understanding should not be interpreted as evidence of one's inadequacy' (Bjork and Yan, 2014, p. 33). Of course, we're looking to incorporate the correct level of difficulty in order for the revision to be effective. The student needs to make an appropriate stretch just beyond their current position – into what evolutionary biologists might call 'the adjacent possible'. We're not looking for hardness for hardness' sake.

4. Testing is central, but that doesn't mean we have to design more tests

Although the importance of practice tests couldn't manifest more clearly in the work of Dunlosky et al. (2013), it doesn't mean we need to respond to this revelation with panic. ('We have to set another [insert appropriately large number] of tests? How are we going to find the time to design and build them? Do we run them from Teams or the VLE? Who's going to mark them?'). Students need to test themselves. Five ways in which this might happen are: (1) we encourage students to revise in pairs and use the time to test each other; (2) we teach them to use flash cards the way flash cards should be used – that is, steering them away from writing on both sides and perhaps using the Leitner Box (Activity 28 in *The A Level Mindset*), so the cards become resources to test recall and explanation; (3) students design their own tests, as suggested in Test Your Future Self (Activity 28) or, in the list of high-practice behaviours below, we're thinking in particular of item 16; (4) students drop a section of text into an AI programme and ask it to set them a test based on the material; or (5) they use the Closed Book Note-Taking technique described in Activity 26.

5. The three T's

The three T's is an idea that has become increasingly central to the way we support students in developing their revision, but there's only so much room in a book like this and we've had to leave it out of the activities. Here it is in a nutshell. We've been exploring the ways in which students mentally organise test questions, and there seem to be – at least in the early stages of our work – three ways in which students group these questions. The first, *topic*, is indicative of lower levels of practice. Here, students only conceive of questions as representative (or not) of a topic, and their questions – and subsequent thoughts – are organised in that way. Those questions that fall outside of topic areas, or seem in any way atypical, are a threat. The next T represents something much more sophisticated; it's *toughness*. Students operating at this level group questions according to how well they can currently answer them. They've got an easy/medium/hard or red/amber/green (RAG)-rated system of revisits going on – and they administer tests for harder topics more regularly. It's an encouraging sign. Finally, and most sophisticated of the three, is *task*. Here, students are focused on command verbs, and are thinking deeply about the skills they need to demonstrate as they solve problems under timed conditions. For a closer examination of this approach, have a look at The Command Verb Table (Activity 30).

Twenty High-Practice Behaviours

Whenever we stumble across a high-practice student, we eagerly gather together what it is they think and do differently, listening out for those replicable tricks or tactics so we can steal them.

Here are the most commonly discussed behaviours we see when we're interviewing high-practice students:

1 I analyse where I have gone wrong on exam or test questions by going through the feedback or checking a mark scheme.

2 I collect exam questions and organise them into groups: topic by topic or easy/medium/hard.

3 I do past paper questions, often for short intense bursts, dipping in and out like mini exams.

4 I have a go at making my own exam-style questions and marking my answers.

5 I have identified my weaker areas of understanding and focused more time on these areas.

6 I know how long each exam is, and I am driven to know how long I will need to spend on each section. I time myself on each section to try to work this out.

7 I know the different command words to expect in a test or exam and have listed them so I can revise each one.

8 I know the skills required in exams and tests; often, I've practised using a range of unfamiliar data, photos, graphs, maps, questions, etc. so it doesn't matter if the wording is different on the day or examples are unfamiliar.

9 I know what I need to do with my notes to make them fit for retrieval/revision, and I spend time regularly checking that I can recall them.

10 I like looking at model answers to understand how to reach the top of the mark scheme.

11 I often lecture my notes out loud from memory, as if I were teaching a class, to practise the kind of explanation the exam will require of me.

12 I reuse past paper questions, sometimes over and over, until I'm confident.

13 I seek out additional exam questions and mark schemes, even if they're from different exam boards.

14 I set myself timed questions and work under exam conditions even when I don't feel like it.

15 I sometimes submit extra work for marking to ensure my teacher gives me a clear steer on how to improve.

16 I sometimes try and 'think like an examiner' – imagining what possible questions might come up for a topic and listing them all.

17 I use flash cards to test my memory, covering up the information and trying to recall it out loud rather than simply covering both sides with notes that I just passively reread.

18 I will find opportunities to test myself on the knowledge I have gained by covering up information from textbooks or class notes and trying to recall it.

19 If there are gaps in my knowledge, I know it's my job to find out how to fill them.

20 When I revise with my friends, we test each other rather than just copy each other's notes.

How might a list like this be useful? You could, of course, use any or all of the approaches we've suggested so far – they'd all work well here. But here's a separate suggestion.

Clarify behaviours by term, cohort or key stage

Rather than ask students to consider all twenty behaviours – it can be a lot to take on if they've tried very few of them in the past – one way to prioritise them might be to break them down chronologically, so the students are asked to develop them in bursts across shorter time periods.

One way you might do this is take the list of twenty behaviours – or, indeed, consider all one hundred – and ask a team of tutors to sequence them from those that operate as 'basic requirements' and need to be embedded immediately and those that qualify as 'advanced'. Your term one study habits might be those you want discussed and experimented with early on, term two might add a layer of sophistication or development and term three might up the challenge further.

The same might work for targeted cohorts. One of our shorter lists – culled from the one hundred, with statements from every element of the VESPA model – is this one, aimed at what we refer to as 'ceiling students' – learners whose previous academic performance suggests we should be seeing more from them but whose habits and approaches are stifling further growth.

With a list like this, we could work more closely with the students and their parents, highlighting the specific behaviours we think might be best at breaking the ceiling.

1 I seek extra material (textbooks, articles, handouts, revision sites) to deepen my understanding of a topic.

2 I can increase periods of concentration if I have to; I know what my main distractions are and how to turn them off so I can focus.

3 I generally know in advance what I plan to achieve in a study session rather than start it and just hope.

4 I go looking for problems – seeking out topics I find hard and listing the questions I want to discuss with my teacher.

5 I set myself little tasks, like reading over the previous week's notes, and try to find the answer to things I don't understand.

6 I can summarise and reshape information so it feels like mine. I might rewrite it or use a table, chart, graph or mind-map.

7 I know what has been covered so far on my course, and ensure it's all there by checking my books against study websites, textbooks or knowledge organisers.

8 I often plan my week in advance, making mini lists of tasks I have to do at the start of particular periods – like on a Monday or over a weekend.

9 I pack my bag for the next day the night before.

10 I do past paper questions, often for short intense bursts, dipping in and out like mini exams.

11 I will find opportunities to test myself on the knowledge I have gained by covering up information and trying to recall it.

12 I expect to have setbacks as part of my learning process. I try to take responsibility for them rather than blame everyone else.

13 I generally focus on written feedback rather than the grade alone.

14 I seek help and support from peers and teachers when needed; I don't feel this is a sign of weakness.

15 I don't allow negative thoughts to dominate; I try to express them in a more positive way: 'One thing this teaches me is …' or 'I know now that next time I need to …' or 'Mistakes give me information on how to improve.'

The same might go for a key stage, with behaviours picked for each term of the year, like this Year 7 example:

Year 7	Elements of the model and accompanying statements	Themes
	Vision 1 If the teacher suggests an out-of-class activity or opportunity, I consider it. 2 I sometimes approach teachers for suggestions for additional reading. 3 I often talk to my friends about my subjects. 4 I want teachers to say good things about me at parents' evenings. 5 I try to get involved in school life, building relationships that will help me as I go along.	Getting involved, buying into culture and expectations.
	Effort 1 My attendance and punctuality are very good. 2 I have a space to work where I can concentrate and focus without interruptions.	Staying engaged.
	Systems 1 My workspace is organised with everything in its place. 2 I have a checklist for the day's tasks and reminders, and tick them off as I go. 3 I file my notes in the right place at the end of each day. 4 I pack my bag for the next day the night before.	Basic organisational techniques, filing and checklisting.

Year 7	Elements of the model and accompanying statements	Themes
	Practice 1 I use textbook questions and exam questions to practise the things I find hard. 2 When I revise with my friends, we test each other rather than just copy each other's notes.	Testing myself, finding the edge of my ability.
	Attitude 1 I allow myself time to be disappointed if something hasn't gone as well as I hoped, but I can move forward and channel it into something practical. 2 I enjoy learning; I try to do my best to enjoy school. 3 I try to be positive, help others to be positive and choose positive friends.	Handling setbacks, positivity, optimism.

25. Practice Activity: High and Low Utility

John Dunlosky, professor of psychology at Kent State University, has closely examined a wide range of practice techniques, then assessed what impact they have on student performance (Dunlosky et al., 2013). Those techniques that seem to have only a weak connection with getting a good grade, he calls 'low utility' techniques. These are necessary at times, but have only a small impact on success. Others he classifies as 'moderate utility' or 'high utility'. These are the techniques that seem to have a very strong association with good exam performance and good grades.

His findings are outlined in the table below – we've adjusted his language to make it more accessible.

Why not make a quick analysis of which techniques you use? Be totally honest. It's not a problem if you only use a few – that describes the vast majority of students in the country.

	Technique	**Always use**	**Sometimes use**	**Never use**
High utility	Practice tests – moving in and out of exam conditions, practising recall or executing on the skills required in the time you're given.			
	Spaced practice – scheduling practice tests and revision sessions out over time; snacking instead of bingeing.			
Moderate utility	Elaborative interrogation – explaining complex concepts and ideas to others, teaching someone else the material.			
	Self-explanation – writing out explanations and explaining how new information is linked to old information. Clarifying connections between information.			

	Technique	Always use	Sometimes use	Never use
Low utility	Interleaved practice – designing study that moves you from topic to topic, task to task and subject to subject rather than blocking out long sessions of the same activity.			
	Summarising – writing out/recording summaries of the information you need to learn.			
	Highlighting – reading material with a highlighter and selecting the key information as you go.			
	Mnemonics – creating phrases, memorable words, visualisations or lists to recollect material.			
	Text into image – attempting to turn information into images to better recall it.			
	Rereading – setting out all your notes and course textbooks and reading them through again.			

Which ones are you routinely doing a lot of? Which ones do you try rarely or never? Choose one technique that is moderate or high utility and try to break it down into steps. What things might you have to do in what order to use the technique effectively?

A healthy balance

We're not saying that you should abandon all low-utility tasks. These tasks work well in the early stages of revision when you're collecting and organising your material.

The problem comes when we continually use these approaches all the way up to the exam. As the exam draws nearer, you need to be trying out the high-utility revision tasks. By incorporating more high-utility strategies into your revision, you'll make more progress in the same amount of time, getting more out of each session by making it harder.

High-utility strategies aren't always easy and they don't always feel comfortable, but they drive you forward faster than the low-utility strategies.

Aim for a healthy balance!

26. Practice Activity: Closed Book Note-Taking

Here's a fascinating study: two psychologists working in Indiana in the United States studied four revision techniques and their impact on test performance (Karpicke and Blunt, 2011).

The students were split into four groups before the test:

1 Single-reading study – in this group, students had to read a chapter once.

2 Repeat-reading study – in this group, students had to read a chapter four times.

3 Mind-mapping – in this group, students read the text once and then summarised it in a mind-map.

4 Active recall – in this group, students read the text once, then covered it up and tested their recall by writing out as much of it as they could remember in two practice tests.

Before they began the experiment, the researchers asked the eighty science students taking part to predict which group would perform best on the subsequent test. What do you think the students predicted would be the most effective technique?

You know that activities like these have surprise punchlines, so you're probably guessing the students were wrong. And they were. So, in the light of that, what is *your* guess as to the technique that was most efficient?

Let's take this a step further.

Two types of question were asked in the test, which were mixed up so the students didn't know what to expect. Type 1 were *recall* questions. Students had to answer simple questions about the information that had appeared in the text. Type 2 were *inference* questions. These questions were harder, asking students to connect ideas and concepts, requiring deeper knowledge.

Now, guess which techniques yielded which results for the simpler recall questions:

	Which technique?
Winners: 65% of questions correct	
Runners-up: 45% of questions correct	
Third place: 40% of questions correct	
Last place: 27% of questions correct	

For the more complex inference questions:

	Which technique?
Winners: 70% of questions correct	
Runners-up: 57% of questions correct	
Third place: 55% of questions correct	
Last place: 28% of questions correct	

The same technique won both times: active recall. It was the one that the students thought would work least well of the four, but in fact it worked the best! It just goes to show that our instincts about revision are often wrong.

Testing yourself will lead to better performance than rereading notes *four times*. Think of the time you could save!

So, active recall is definitely a technique you should add to your repertoire. A great way of incorporating active recall into your studies is to try closed book note-taking.

An Active Recall Study Technique in Five Steps

First, you'll need to choose something you want to learn. You'll need a section of textbook (not too long), a study guide or some notes you've already made. Once you've chosen what you're aiming to learn, here's what to do:

1 Read the section of textbook/information *while highlighting the key information.* Really connect and concentrate as you read and highlight.

2 Now close the book/put the notes away.

3 Now write notes on the section you've just covered without looking at the information. It will feel hard. You might get frustrated. You won't be able to remember everything. No problem; leave lots of space to add forgotten information. Scatter the notes around the page using subheadings and leave lots of white paper.

4 When you're done, open the book or turn over the notes. Reread and note-take as you go but …

5 Add the stuff you missed or forgot in another colour, filling the white space you left the first time around.

That's it! This approach will be more effective than reading the material four times. You might even finish more quickly than you would have rereading the information four times.

Of course, it will feel harder than just rereading. It's not as comfortable and you might feel exhausted by the end. But, you'll perform better in tests and exams if you make this part of your weekly study.

27. Practice Activity: Verbal Recaps

This tool is a habit-changer which will very quickly boost your understanding. Of all the activities in this chapter, it's the one that takes only a little effort but can yield big results – so it's well worth a try next time you have something you need to read.

Here's what you do. Every time you read a page of a textbook or study guide, stop and then:

1. Close the book.
2. Calm your mind for a second and think – what did I just read?
3. Now talk aloud, summarising in your own words exactly what you've just been reading. Choose one of these starters to get you going if it helps:

   » The writer has just been explaining that …

   » This section explores …

   » The important idea here is that …

   » This page outlines the importance of …

   » The writer's argument here is that …

   » I've been reading about how …

   » I've learned that …

4. If you can't summarise it clearly, there's a problem. Not to worry. Go back, read the page again and repeat step 3.
5. Once you're happy that you can summarise the content, try asking and answering more complex questions – not 'what' but 'why' or 'how'. Try these:

   » Why is this section important? Because …

   » Why has it been included? Well, it's crucial because …

   » Why is this bit detailed – or why isn't it detailed? I guess it's because …

» Why is the information in this order? The writer covers this first/second/third because …

» How does it relate to the previous section? It's linked in the following way …

Reading like this means you go slower, but it means you're testing yourself as you go along.

Two Extensions to Try

1. Try adding spoken summaries of whole chapters once you've read them, like this:

First, the writers explore …

Then they go on to argue that …

Then they look at … in more detail, explaining how …

And they finish by concluding that …

You'll find that the information you've read goes in, it sticks and it's easier to recall. Your reading might have taken a little longer, but you've been able to fully explain what it is you've just read.

2. Try putting together a short lecture as if to an imaginary class

We often suggest the following script if you want to have a go at this one. It looks straightforward, but you'll quickly find that you really need to know your topic to start your mini lecture in this way.

It's a good one to do in a study group: each member takes responsibility for one topic and presents it using the script below.

This afternoon, I'm going to be talking you through …

This part of the course is crucial because …

The key definitions you'll need to be able to handle are …

The big ideas that you'll need to be confident about are …

The exam is going to ask you to … so pay particular attention to …

Right, we're ready to get started. A good place to begin this lecture is by looking at …

28. Practice Activity: Test Your Future Self

There are a vast array of academic studies in which researchers have found that one of the all-time superstars of revision techniques is to test your recall. Sometimes this is called active recall – a technique where you deliberately strain the muscles of your memory by trying to remember things you've studied without referring to your notes.

But who sets these tests and where are they? It can be a pain trying to track down tests or search online for just the right kind of test. Instead, we're going to suggest you set yourself the tests.

Hang on, you might be thinking, if I've set the test won't I know the answers straight away? Good point. It's a problem, but here's how to get around it. At the end of a period of study, the last thing you should do is *set a test for your future self*. It should take about ten minutes, and it's a really valuable way to finish a session. By the time you return to the topic, a few days, or even weeks, might have passed and you'll have forgotten precisely what it was you put in your test. But because you're the one who set it, you'll know that the test covers the material perfectly.

What should your test look like? Mostly, that's up to you, but we'd make the following suggestions:

» Use the question, 'If my future self recalled this material perfectly, what would they know?' and make a list of the things to include in your test.

» Start with easy questions and move on to harder ones. Leave the toughest questions until last. These can be the questions that might build on all the others.

» Consider asking definition questions early on, using the words 'what' or 'when' to start your questions. Get the basics sorted.

» Think about moving towards harder question words as you go along. 'How' or 'why' will require your future self to do some explaining, so leave those until the end.

» Consider finishing with a tricky question which replicates something a real exam might ask.

» Make a note of what kind of test score would make you happy with your future self. It doesn't have to be 10/10 – maybe you'll be pleased if you score 7 or above.

And that's it – ten minutes' work which means that the next time you revisit this topic, you can begin with a ready-made test to check what you remember.

Two other things to consider when using this method. First, make a note of your score when you first complete the test. Then come back to the topic again – maybe a week or ten days later – and retake the test. If your score is improving, you can start to feel more confident about that topic.

Second, if you revisit a topic and you're scoring really well on recall, you can leave it for a while and prioritise those topics where you're not doing so well. Or, if you're feeling brave, you can design an ever harder test.

29. Practice Activity: Cog P versus Cog A

A fascinating experiment took place at the University of Georgia led by a professor of biology, Kathrin Stanger-Hall (2012). Students were split into two groups. They were going to be taught the same material by the same teacher using the same resources, but there was the one difference – the first group knew they were going to be tested at the end by a ninety-question multiple-choice exam, and the second group knew they'd take the same multiple-choice exam followed by a more challenging series of short answer questions.

Off they went to revise for their exam. The researchers watched them closely, examining exactly how they studied. It turned out there was no difference in the amount of time they spent studying. However, there was a difference in how they approached their revision.

Those who knew all they had to do was to prepare for a multiple-choice exam became passive learners (we're going to call this group *cog P: cognitively passive*). They tended towards five revision strategies that were comfortable, repetitive and less challenging. Here they are:

1. Reading the assigned text.
2. Rereading class notes.
3. Making flash cards of notes.
4. Highlighting key terms during reading.
5. Looking up difficult information.

Those who knew they also faced short answer questions prepared differently. They were active, testing themselves more regularly and pushing themselves to do harder revision sessions (we're going to call this group *cog A: cognitively active*). Here are five of the activities they used:

1. Repeatedly asking/explaining 'How does it work?' and 'Why does it work this way?'

2. Creating and answering challenging study questions.

3. Closing notes and testing how much they remembered.

4. Drawing and labelling diagrams from memory.

5. Setting tests, trying to answer questions and then looking up information.

Before we show you what happened to their results, think about the differences between these approaches and make some observations or suggestions about the impact they may have had.

The researchers looked just at the responses to the ninety multiple-choice questions because both groups answered these. So, what did they find?

» Cog A students scored significantly higher on these ninety questions.

» Cog A students scored significantly higher on the higher-level questions.

» Cog A students learned significantly more, including critical-thinking skills.

» Of the cog A students, 72.1% agreed or strongly agreed that they saw the value of learning.

» Of the cog P students, 57.3% of students agreed or strongly agreed that they saw the value of learning.

What does this teach us? Cognitively active revision gets you better results, *even if you spend the same amount of time doing it*. This means you might not have to do more revision to be successful; you might just have to do different revision. That's great news for your work–life balance!

Practice

Plan a revision session that incorporates a cognitively active revision technique in the space below.

30. Practice Activity: The Command Verb Table

What do your exams actually ask you to do? We've worked with students who, despite revising hard, aren't fully clear on what to expect on the day of the exam. As a result, they often have a meltdown or go blank. But this doesn't have to be you!

We've gathered nearly one hundred command verbs from different GCSE and A level exam boards, then considered a further fifty command verbs used in professional workplace exams. We've put them all together and tried to group them depending on the types of things they want from us. We're not saying that our groups are perfect, and we're not arguing that any of these groups are 'easier' or 'harder' than the others, but we're pretty sure that most sections of your exams will be summarised in here somewhere, regardless of which subjects you take.

Exams want us to be able to:

1 **Define and describe things.** This could be history dates, people or places, parts of processes, complex vocabulary in full sentences, a foreign language, subject-specific terms, one or two-step processes to solve a sum and so on.

2 **Explain how things work and show that we can use them to solve problems.** This could be describing how the water cycle works, how the heart beats or breathing works, or how something is built, like a poem, a novel or a business. It might be showing that we understand something by using it successfully, like arriving at an answer in maths by following a particular method, showing you know how stories work by writing your own or using grammar correctly in translating a passage from French or German.

3 **Zoom into detail, analysing why things work the way they do.** Here, you might be pulling something apart to zoom in on it – the images in a poem in English or the shape of a river valley in geography. You might be translating and discussing a difficult passage, assessing a big table of data in science and comparing it to what you already know, or solving a complicated problem in maths using a number of steps. Often, you've got two things to handle at once: comparing two advertising campaigns in media or two businesses in economics, or exploring why two characters in a novel are similar or different.

4 **Make judgements about things and justify opinions.** In these questions, you're asked to offer an original opinion of your own. You use what you know to justify your

opinion. You might be using evidence to argue a particular point of view in history or geography. You might be adopting a point of view that isn't yours in sociology and arguing it through. You could be predicting, 'What will happen if …?' in psychology or economics, or making recommendations about increasing profit in business studies, or making judgements about the success or impact of novels or plays.

How did we do, and what have we missed? A great activity would be to go through these descriptions and check them against a standard exam paper. Have we covered some, most or all the questions? If we're not covering everything in this model, what are we missing? What's your fifth or even sixth category?

Each one of these groups tends to come with its own command verbs – words used in the exam that make it clear what type of question it is. We've listed lots that we found below, but you'll find plenty of others you can add to our list.

Command verb table

Define and describe things	**Explain how things work and show that we can use them to solve problems**
Label	Explain
Annotate	Comment on
List	Determine
Define	Demonstrate
Describe	Identify/Infer
Select	Calculate
State/Relate	Show/Prove/Set out
Outline	Verify/Give reasons for/Consider
Summarise	Translate
Illustrate (with examples)	Correct

Zoom into detail, analysing why things work the way they do	**Make judgements about things and justify opinions**
Analyse	Discuss/To what extent
Examine	Evaluate
Explore	Assess
Compare and contrast/Differentiate between/Distinguish between	Argue
	Justify
Survey	Criticise
Review	Suggest/Propose/Make a case for
Investigate	Predict
Solve	Recommend

There are four ways of using the command verb table:

1 Take a subject you're studying and read a whole exam paper from beginning to end. Make a note of what every question is asking you to do, and then see what types you've got. Is it mostly one type? A scattering of types? Is there one area of questions you don't have to worry about at all?

2 Have a look at the distribution of marks. Do certain question types seem to have more marks attached to them? This might tell you what the exam board thinks is important in your answers, and what skills they're less concerned about.

3 Once you've done steps 1 and 2, you can set yourself better tests. You don't need to chase down every exam paper ever published; you can create your own exam that follows the rough shape of other papers. Set and complete your own papers.

4 RAG-rate the question types you're going to face – red for question types you find really hard, amber for those in the middle and green for the type of question you can breeze through. Then adjust your revision so you're spending more time on red question types.

31. Practice Activity: The Overnight Boost

In 2016, a study in Lyon, France, examined students preparing for a test that was all about recall (Mazza et al., 2016). The participants had to learn sixteen words in Swahili – a language they'd never studied before – and remember their translations when asked under exam conditions. So far, so predictable. But here's where the study gets interesting: the students were split into two groups of twenty and given different circumstances in which to revise.

Group 1 were called the 'sleep' group. This lot revised the material at 9pm, then went to sleep and took their test at 9am. Group 2 were the 'wake' group. They revised at 9am, then did their usual day at college/university/work and took their test at 9pm. Both groups were the same in terms of gender, age, quality of sleep and so on, but it quickly became apparent that there were differences in what happened when they sat down to complete their tests.

Exam 1 happened after twelve hours. The students in each group saw the same sixteen words in Swahili and had to type the translations from memory. Exam 2 happened after one week and the same procedure was followed. Exam 3 happened after six months; same procedure again. There was no studying in-between these times.

Why not have a guess at what happened? We've given you a table and added the scores the groups achieved on their first attempt after twelve hours. We've left four missing scores and listed the four numbers you need below the table. All you have to do is match the scores to the correct box.

	Exam 1: Average score out of 16 after twelve hours	**Exam 2:** Average score out of 16 after one week	**Exam 3:** Average score out of 16 after six months
The sleep group	10.3 out of 16		
The wake group	7.5 out of 16		

Other scores achieved: 15.2, 11.3, 8.7, 3.4.*

* Clue (not that you need it!): the 'sleep' group scored better in all the tests.

Once you've decided, have a think about why you've chosen the results you have (assuming you haven't just put them in randomly). Why do you think the results might be happening in the way you have predicted? What variables might be at play here?

The researchers concluded that the sleep group performed better because – and here's a direct quote from the study – 'sleep has been shown both to passively protect memories against decay and interference and to actively consolidate new memories' (Mazza et al., 2016, p. 2). In other words, sleep allows the brain to process and store information without disturbance, strengthening it in your memory.

The sleep group also performed better because the wake group 'operated on memories degraded by interference' (Mazza et al., 2016, p. 8) – in other words, the busy events of the day 'get in the way of' or 'slow down' the brain's ability to process and store information.

What Does All of This Mean for Us?

The study suggests that a good way to tackle a subject or topic that won't stick in your head is to try what we call the 'overnight boost' to crack it. Here's how an overnight boost works:

» Just like in the experiment, revise your hard-to-remember topic in the evening. Spend two short twenty-five-minute bursts on it, with absolutely no distractions. Read it through actively. Make clear, simple notes in bullet point form capturing the main information. The session doesn't have to be at 9pm like the experiment, but you want as little further stimulus as possible after the work. Try to do it close to bedtime. Avoid watching TV or doing any further work after your session. Just pack away, take it easy and then sleep.

» In the morning, about ten hours later if you can, test the material from memory. Take out your notes, quickly scan through the main points and then cover everything up. You're going to push yourself to recall it all from memory. Speak it out loud or write it down like a test.

That's it! Stick with the strategy and pretty soon you'll find that the information is really embedding in your thinking and your recollection is getting stronger and stronger.

32. Practice Activity: Sticky Timetables

Educational researcher Douglas Barton, the founder of Elevate Education, delivered an interesting TED talk about revision, using data his organisation has collected to identify which revision activities have the biggest impact on exam performance (Barton, 2015). If you've read any of our other practice activities, you won't be surprised to find that the winner was 'practice exams'. However, another high-impact activity was 'designing and sticking to a revision timetable'.

The trouble is, Barton says, huge proportions of students don't stick to the schedule they've designed. He's interviewed those students who abandon their timetables to find out why. His conclusion? They design them incorrectly.

So, what is the mistake they make? They start by putting in the slots when they're going to work, and then try to fit real life around these revision sessions. As a result, these students create days and weeks that are dominated by revision, while activities that might bring them joy, happiness, relaxation or connection are squeezed out. It becomes impossible to sustain and, before long, they consign the timetable to the bin.

Designing Sticky Timetables

We think there are five things to focus on when creating a successful timetable. Have a go at designing one for yourself now. You don't need anything fancy, and the internet is bursting with templates. Anyway, as you know, it's not the template that's going to make the difference; it's these five steps.

1 **Start by putting some key moments of connection, joy and relaxation into your week.** Aim for five or six moments of between one and two hours (totalling about ten or twelve hours) when you're doing something rewarding. Consider taking part in sports, going to the gym, watching TV, meeting up with friends or a shift in a part-time job. Organise these activities so they're not happening all at once. You might have an hour on a Monday when you meet a friend, ninety minutes on a Wednesday when you watch a football match, an hour on Thursday to go for a run and relax, pizza night on Friday or a period of time on Saturday to go into town.

2 **Now begin to organise the work slots around these periods of relaxation.** Check carefully that your relaxation slots aren't crowding out your work. You're aiming for balance, so you've got plenty of time to do the work you need to do, but you've also got these moments of celebration and freedom to keep you going.

3 **Mentally rehearse the week, thinking about 'mission' and 'medal'.** Run through your week in your head. You're aiming for a week that feels challenging but doable; that will ensure you do plenty of revision but a moment of relaxation or joy is never far away. For every tough period of revision, you need a reward (a mission then a medal) – something small like a fifteen-minute break and a snack, a twenty-minute sitcom episode or a playlist of uplifting tunes that's only three songs long. Also look at your longer periods of relaxation and joy. If your week doesn't feel quite right in your head, identify tricky periods – is there too much relaxation happening all at once? Is there a run of three days that's solid revision and needs breaking up?

4 **Run it through once and then adjust.** It could be the figures we've mentioned here aren't right for you, and that's fine. With each completed week, you've got a chance to redesign your timetable. This is going to be a flexible and constantly changing document that responds to your progress and levels of energy.

5 **Ignore the setbacks.** There's going to be a day when you don't follow your timetable. Guaranteed. If this happens, don't beat yourself up. Just start again tomorrow as if nothing has gone wrong!

As courses get harder and workload increases, students who consider willpower a limited resource experience self-regulation failure and begin to procrastinate.

5. Attitude

Attitude: the settled beliefs students have about their role in the learning process, their own capabilities and the part they play in the development of those capabilities.

What Do We See When Attitude is Low?

Our habits of mind are determined by so many things; we pick them up from our family structures, we copy behaviours from older siblings, we might mirror the behaviours of our peers or reproduce attitudes we see in the media. But these attitudes, values and habits of mind can change. Often, this change is slow and characterised by inconsistency – for example, we might see a falling back into old ways of thinking when times are tough. However, with patience, empathy and positivity, we can slowly but surely change the way students see the world around them and, in time, their behaviours too.

When attitude is low, we'll see clues that might include some or all of the following: students' self-talk might be insistently negative. They might refer to themselves as 'stupid' or consider themselves doomed to fail. They might escape the intense discomfort of these thoughts by suppressing them rather than recasting them – attempting to avoid situations in which the self-talk is proved correct. That might mean missing a test on purpose and finding reasons not to take it in their own time, or ignoring your instruction to 'Work under timed conditions for thirty minutes on this, handwritten, and submit whatever you managed to achieve' and opt instead for three neatly typed pages that take hours to complete. They might be plagued by perfectionism, with any evidence of errors or slip-ups being confirmation that they're not capable.

Or they might take an entirely different approach to tackling negative self-talk, embracing and revelling in it. We might see some low-attitude students publicly and noisily declare that they haven't done any work, make fun of those who have or refer to ambitious students as 'try-hards'. Counterintuitively, for these 'need to avoid failure' students (see Activity 33: NAF and NACH), the way of avoiding failure is to make it inevitable and then explain it away ('I didn't try, and I don't care anyway'). Low-attitude students might have a fixed mindset or compare themselves negatively to others ('Everyone else is cleverer than me'). They might consider asking for help as evidence that they're intellectually inferior, so avoid following up on areas of confusion or attempting to solve any of their own study problems. They often consider feedback as a description of themselves rather than their work, so rarely read feedback or act on it, interpreting it as a slight ('My teacher hates me'). Finally, we might see students who feel they have no agency or control over their own lives ('The government will choose my grade in the end, so what's the point?').

Changing patterns of thinking like this is a long game. We might be only transient influences in the lives of low-attitude students, doing our bit to model and encourage more positive thinking, and never seeing our work bear fruit as the student moves on. But that doesn't make the attempt any less important.

Research Spotlight: What the Evidence Indicates

A lot of studies into attitude, unsurprisingly, focus on self-beliefs about cognitive performance. There is a large body of research pointing to the importance of self-belief in academic success; often, concepts are subdivided and studied separately, so you can read about self-efficacy (Albert Bandura pioneered this work; in a fascinating paper published in the 1980s, he takes students who are 'phobic' about particular subjects and measures their increasing levels of self-efficacy as they gradually improve their tests scores (Bandura, 1982)), mindset (for a helpful summary of Carol Dweck's famous work, try her 2019 paper, 'Mindsets: A View From Two Eras', co-written with David Yeager), buoyancy or self-confidence. On the latter,

Lazar Stankov, Suzanne Morony and Yim Ping Lee found that students' confidence – conceptually close to self-efficacy in models of self-belief – had the strongest correlation with performance in maths tests, for example (Stankov et al., 2014).

But one of our favourite studies, which is connected to education and included here because it confounds and delights, is Alia Crum and Ellen Langer's (2007) study of hotel cleaners. The researchers were interested in the potential that attitude might have on weight loss, so they studied eighty-four female room attendants working across seven different hotels. Just over half – forty-four subjects – were taught how physically demanding their jobs were; how much exercise they were getting as they cleaned an average of fifteen rooms a day, each taking between twenty and thirty minutes of 'walking, bending, pushing, lifting, and carrying' (Crum and Langer, 2007, p. 6). They were given calorie-expenditure information for their typical activities, so they knew that vacuuming for a certain amount of time burned a certain number of calories, for example. The control group, on the other hand, received no teaching at all. The subjects went off to perform their usual tasks. Their workload remained constant in the interim, their self-reported exercise outside of work didn't change and their diets remained the same. They were all weighed and measured thirty days later.

If this investigation sounds far-fetched, Crum and Langer were following a precedent. Almost fifteen years earlier, Robert Desharnais and colleagues at California State University, Los Angeles had put forty-eight adults on a ten-week exercise programme. Half were told it was about well-being and were given associated information, the other half didn't. Fitness increased in both groups to the same extent, but when the well-being of the two groups was assessed, the group who had been told the programme was designed to increase well-being showed a significant improvement in their self-esteem (Decharnais et al., 1993). Other studies have shown that the way we perceive and describe our own health – effectively *the health story we tell ourselves* – is a better predictor of longevity than our actual health (Kaplan and Camacho, 1983).

So, Crum and Langer's hypothesis, that 'mindset mediates the connection between exercise and health' (Crum and Langer, 2007, p. 5), doesn't sound so unusual in this context. And so it proved. The group who were taught that they were exercising well by simply engaging in their work began to report they were exercising more. There was no change in the time they spent exercising, simply a change in awareness. As the authors point out, these changes are 'attributable not to actual increases in physical activity, but to a shift in mindset initiated by the information given to them in the intervention'. They also went on to lose more weight – roughly two pounds – than the control group, as well as lowering their blood pressure by 10%, improving their body mass index and having 'significantly healthier levels of body fat' than the control (Crum and Langer, 2007, p. 13). 'Of course,' the researchers conclude, 'it is possible that the room attendants actually did change their behavior – actually did cut back on calories, improved food quality, or worked harder or more energetically – but *did not report it*' (Crum and Langer, 2007, p. 14; original emphasis). It seems unlikely that this would happen independently to all forty-four participants, but even if it had, it would say something interesting about the power of teaching on mindset and behaviour.

In a study involving classroom learning, we get a vivid illustration of the power of attitudinal posture on academic behaviour. Veronika Job at the University of Vienna outlines two opposing attitudes about willpower: first, that willpower is a limited resource that needs to be carefully assigned – we feel depleted and make poor decisions as our willpower becomes exhausted, and, second, that willpower is an unlimited resource that can be self-generating (Job et al., 2015). Job argues that rather than testing willpower in a laboratory setting, we should be using 'real-world settings in which people contend with accumulating demands on their self-control as they strive to accomplish personal goals' (Job et al., 2015, p. 7). So, Job followed 176 university students week by week across a whole academic term. First, she established which attitudinal group the students belonged to – whether they saw willpower as exhaustible (she calls it 'limited theory') or self-generating – and she also collected measures of the students' perceived levels of self-control. Then, she and her team sent regular questionnaires for the students to answer as the term went on. The questions asked them about current workload, tendency towards procrastination, poor time management, anticipated demands such as submissions or upcoming presentations, and even their spending patterns and unhealthy eating.

The findings are a compelling snapshot of the impact of attitude on behaviour. There was no difference between the students when workload was low, but as the course got harder and workload increased, the students who considered willpower a limited resource experienced self-regulation failure and began to procrastinate. When there were a lot of demands on them, students whose conception of willpower was limited found it harder to get down to work and even consumed more unhealthy foods. Job went on to collect end-of-term academic grades and the findings were equally interesting: those students who believed willpower was limited had lower academic scores (even when controlled for previous scores). 'Students who endorsed the limited theory and who faced high demands over the term,' Job writes, 'procrastinated more' and 'earned lower grades than students with the nonlimited-resource theory … because they were more likely to procrastinate in completing their work' (Job et al., 2015, p. 21). It raises the question that if we could teach students that their willpower was self-generating, we might, over time, begin to change their attitudes and so their behaviours.

When We're Working with Students …

As we've mentioned in previous chapters, simply urging students to think differently won't work. Instead, making them feel more normal is an important step; acknowledging that, 'Yes, study can be hard and it can feel impossible, but the period you're going through now has been successfully navigated by thousands of students across the UK and abroad just one year ago. They all felt like this too – and they got through it. So will you.'

Here are a few issues, concepts and approaches which might help to frame the activities that follow:

1. Cheerleading doesn't have the impact we might hope.

Tempting as it is to deliver an impassioned speech – 'You're better than you think, you can do this!' – we might have to first acknowledge where the student is at currently.

2. Modelling vulnerability plays an important role.

We've found that deliberately lowering our status and sharing vulnerability around work has been useful. Try, 'I remember feeling exactly the same way,' or 'I once had a really tricky study problem and ended up dreading going into school,' or 'It's a tough time of year for staying upbeat, isn't it? I feel the same. Here's something I've been trying recently …' Low-attitude students, with their tendency to compare themselves unfavourably to others, often assume that everyone else is getting along fine with their studies and no one else is unhappy or struggling. Telling a student, 'It's quite normal to feel the way you are. This time last year, I spoke to lots of students who said exactly what you have,' can help to normalise low periods. (If you're interested in exploring this further, Activity 38: The Change Curve, in *The A Level Mindset*, might be a good starting point.)

3. Exploring the idea that attention is something we have control over has proved useful for us.

We've been impressed by Winifred Gallagher's *Rapt* (2010) on this topic. Gallagher writes about how our 'top-down attention' – that is, the proportion of our attention that isn't our instinctive, scanning-for-danger, hunter-gatherer attention – is controllable. That we essentially choose what to pay attention to, and our brains have developed to have a small, manageable attentional spotlight. In other words, we select details from the world around us, foregrounding certain things and filtering out the rest. What we pay attention to can be a matter of habit. Do we remember only the negative things from a day at school or college, or can we force ourselves to dwell on the positives instead? (There are two activities among the eight that follow that will help students do this. Think Three Positives (Activity 38), for example, is an activity we've done regularly with groups of students as well as with our own children.)

4. Recasting negative thinking can be learned.

When we're discussing study with low-attitude students, it's important to model the use of emotion-free descriptors of the current situation. If we're sitting with a student who's failing a course, we can simply say, 'OK, so your currently estimated grade is a 3.' No judgement, no inflating of cheeks and raising of eyebrows, no implied criticism and certainly no, 'It's all a bit of a mess, isn't it?' Once you've modelled reasoned, balanced language, try collecting a student's observations on a situation and reading them back: 'So you're saying – I'm using your own words here – that "everything is falling apart". Can we look at some evidence for this feeling?' We're taking an objective and non-judgemental position before showing how else we might express that feeling. 'So when you say, "everything is falling apart", you mean you've "fallen behind in your submission of work and need a period in which you can catch up without getting told off". Does that sound about right?'

5. Examples of other students asking for help have been really useful for us.

If you want, anonymise them and add some distance using stories of previous students: 'I was working with a student very similar to you last year. They ended up making this decision to speak to their teachers and ask for advice. They didn't feel comfortable at first, but it really worked for them.' Or, 'I'm seeing a lot of students at the moment asking exactly the same as you are, and here's what

I've been encouraging them to do …' List all the sources of help that are available to the student, and ask them to consider if each one is a resource they've taken advantage of. 'So, you've never stayed behind after class to ask a teacher a question? You might be missing a trick there. I know lots of other students, many of them just like you, who've started doing that. And the difference to their confidence has been great to see.' Or you might try, 'If we wanted to get this problem solved more quickly, could we call in a favour from someone?' Patiently pursuing this agenda normalises asking for support. We often find high-attitude students do it far more often than their low-attitude peers, and we can correct that.

Twenty High-Attitude Behaviours

Whenever we're working with a high-attitude student, someone optimistic and resourceful, someone who both expects and solves study problems and doesn't take feedback too personally, we gather together what it is they think and do differently. As with other elements of the VESPA model, we're looking for the replicable tricks or tactics so that we can move beyond 'stay positive' or 'believe in yourself' next time we're working with a learner whose beliefs are potentially limiting their progress.

Here are the most commonly discussed behaviours we see when we're interviewing high-attitude students:

1 I allow myself time to be disappointed if something hasn't gone as well as I hoped, but I can move forward and make a list of what I need to improve.

2 I can allow myself to be proud of what I have achieved, making a note of good news so I can return to it when I'm feeling less positive.

3 I don't allow negative thoughts to dominate. I try to express them in a more positive way; 'One thing this teaches me is …' or 'I know now that next time I need to …'

4 I expect to have setbacks as part of my learning process. I try to take responsibility for them rather than blame everyone else.

5 I generally focus on written feedback rather than the mark or grade alone because that is where the advice will be. I read it carefully and use it to redraft work if I'm unhappy.

6 I have some tactics I use if I'm feeling demotivated – go for a run, walk my dog, visit my friend or take a break.

7 I know constructive feedback is not an attack on my personality, and this helps me to action it rather than ignore it.

8 I know that my brain is changing as I challenge myself, and I remind myself of things I can do now that I couldn't before.

9 I know that feedback is sometimes a reflection on my levels of effort or concentration. If I have to, I will accept that I need to do more.

10 I remind myself that no one will remember the marks I get during the course – it will be the mark at the end that matters – so I will generally give challenging work a go and try not to be afraid of making errors.

11 I see my peers' strengths as an opportunity to learn from them – for example, by asking to revise as a pair, swapping notes or checking someone else's work.

12 I seek help and support from peers and teachers when needed; I don't feel this is a sign of weakness.

13 I sometimes force myself to be positive – for example, by listing three good things that have recently happened.

14 I try to be positive, help others to be positive and choose positive friends. When friends get overly negative, I either tell them or take a break from them.

15 I try not to feel embarrassed when I'm praised but accept the praise and reflect on why it was given.

16 I try to remind myself that 'mistakes are information' – that when something goes wrong, it gives me a chance to analyse why it went wrong and what I can do to improve.

17 I try to use caring language and positive self-talk to discuss my learning; even when things have been hard, I try not to criticise myself.

18 I visualise qualities like willpower and self-control as endless rather than imagine I have a limited amount that will run out; it helps me to think and reflect, and to make better decisions in the moment.

19 When I improve a score or mark, I take time to recognise what I did to achieve it – perhaps making a note so I can make sure that I repeat my success.

20 When I need to, I know I can focus on how far I've come and reassure myself that I'm making progress.

How might a list like this be useful? You could, of course, use any or all of the approaches we've suggested under the other four elements of the model; they're all entirely interchangeable. But here's our fifth suggestion.

Ask students to coach others

Professor Katy Milkman, an economist at The Wharton School of the University of

Pennsylvania and the former president of the Society of Judgment and Decision Making, writes powerfully about the saying-is-believing effect in her book *How to Change* (2021). We were particularly struck by her argument that coaching improves the coach as well as the coachee; that through a combination of effects, such as increased clarity of thinking as well as increased levels of self-confidence, student coaches can improve their study skills even as they support others.

It works well with students who are showing signs of improvement in study but would still benefit from some positive affirmation of their progress and potential. You might ask them to go through all one hundred behaviours we've suggested, picking out the ones they feel best qualified to explore in preparation for a conversation with a student from the year group below them, for example.

33. Attitude Activity: NAF and NACH

According to need achievement theory, first developed by psychologists David McClelland and John Atkinson, different personality types emerge when we attempt something testing or competitive. The theory is complex, but sports psychology often summarises it as two opposing positions referred to as NAF and NACH:

1 **Need to avoid failure (NAF).** These people tend to avoid challenges because they don't want to risk failing. They are sometimes slow workers who avoid responsibility. In class, they can be easily dissuaded from taking part or finishing a piece of work and don't like being assessed. They may want to be successful, but the fear of failure outweighs the desire to succeed. This means they will avoid situations where they might fail, by not handing work in or telling everybody how little work they have done.

2 **Need to achieve (NACH).** These are the people who thrive on challenge. They are usually determined workers who take risks and enjoy being assessed. Failure isn't a problem for these people. If they get a low score or a disappointing grade, they'll take it in their stride and move on. The desire to be successful outweighs the fear of failure, so even though they feel some fear, they still put themselves in situations where they might fail.

Last year, which were you?

We're all changing all the time – we can be NAF one day and NACH another. And since it's often easier to reflect on a period of time just passed, ask yourself: did you have a tendency towards one of these stances last year? Which one? How did it affect your behaviour and grades?

This year, which are you?

Although we can change ourselves, we often get into habits of mind which mean we carry on doing the things we always have. Are you different this year, or the same?

Now ...

Imagine you are a teacher trying to decide whether your students are NAFs or NACHs. Here's a list of behaviours you might see in your class. Do you think the student is a NAF or a NACH?

- This student is struggling with understanding the work but won't ask questions in class to clarify their learning. When you ask why, they say they 'feel embarrassed'.
- You gave this student a low grade for a piece of work two lessons ago. They arrive this lesson with the piece of work redone and ask if you'd mind marking it again.
- When you organise some group work, this student asks to work with a group of students who are doing much better than they are.
- This student will often tell others, 'I haven't revised for this test' or 'I'd forgotten we were having this exam.'
- These two students, who are struggling with the content of this topic, ask a lot of questions during and after class ('Can you explain that again?' 'What do you mean?'), even when other students roll their eyes and tut.
- These two students are both struggling and prefer to sit with each other, often talking about other things.

You might be able to define some further behaviours associated with NAF and NACH. Use the table below to capture a few more.

NAF behaviours	**NACH behaviours**
....	....
....	....
....	....
....	....

A Commitment

Now take two or three NACH behaviours you might not be doing currently. Choose ones that look possible – the kind of thing you could integrate into your working week – and make a commitment to give them a try.

Really commit to them. If they feel uncomfortable, do it for a short time period, so you can try it out.

You'll find small things begin to change. You might make more errors, but those errors generate a new understanding that takes you forward. You might find that you do a little more independent work than normal. Or you might find that your confidence increases slightly.

These small changes might not have an immediate impact, but they could be the start of your grades improving!

34. Attitude Activity: Check Ahead, Check Back

Comparison is the thief of joy.

The quote above, often erroneously attributed to US president Theodore Roosevelt, suggests that if we compare ourselves to others, we may find ourselves unhappy.

It sounds like common sense, except perhaps it isn't always the case. It's true that sometimes we can make ourselves miserable by comparing ourselves to people we think have it better than us, but at other times we can make ourselves feel better by comparing ourselves to those in less fortunate positions – including our previous selves or previous generations.

Consider this:

» In the lottery of birth you got a winning ticket.

» You've been brought up in a country free from war or geological disaster. You don't have to worry about conflict or persecution.

» What's more, you were born in the twenty-first century. There is clean water, food, warmth and shelter. There are rights and freedoms of which your grandparents could only have dreamed. Plus, round-the-clock internet access.

» And you're a successful learner with a healthy and developing brain. You can read, write, pass high-stakes exams, absorb new information, follow your country's breakneck twenty-four-hour news cycle, swim, maybe even drive or ride a bike, master tricky computer games, build flatpack furniture, cook a little bit, maybe skateboard, dance, use a MacBook Pro …

Having read that, hopefully, you're feeling just a little bit better! When it's well-used, comparison can be a useful tool. We just have to be careful about when it's best to *check ahead* (seeing what's on the road ahead – the challenges we've still got to face and the people we think might be further along than us) or *check back* (reminding ourselves how far we've come and considering how lucky we are and what progress we've made).

It's well worth assessing your current state of mind, then choosing which column you might explore in more detail.

Check ahead	Check back
Best done when: you're feeling stable and confident, you're optimistic and ready for a challenge. **Questions you might ask yourself:** What three challenges are coming up soon? What do I need to be ready for? Who is ahead of me at the moment? What is one thing they are better at than me? What technique could I learn by looking at how they do things? What qualities or characteristics have they got that I would like to cultivate? How do they approach their work?	**Best done when:** you're feeling like you've struggled through a few setbacks and you're doubting your ability. **Questions you might ask yourself:** What has been the hardest thing I've achieved so far? If I had to choose three things I'm proud of myself for, what would they be? What didn't I know a month ago that I know now? A term ago? A year ago? What couldn't I do in Year 11 that I've mastered now? Who is less fortunate than me, and what might I do to help them?

Healthy comparison is about knowing what you need psychologically. On some days, we need the reassurance and comfort of checking back and seeing everything we've achieved and how far we've come. On other days, we might need a wake-up call – a moment when we get ready for and enthusiastic about the hard work ahead. Try this activity if you feel in need of either!

35. Attitude Activity: A Dozen Noticeboards

There's a research team at Hertfordshire University called the Perrott-Warrick Research Unit headed by Richard Wiseman. They are interested in luck and how/why people who consider themselves 'lucky' or 'unlucky' get to be that way.

Wiseman wrote a book called *The Luck Factor* (2003) about his findings. Four hundred volunteers who considered themselves particularly lucky or unlucky were asked to complete a series of experiments. In one, the subjects were given a newspaper to flip through and a task: to count the number of photographs in the newspaper. Three pages in, there was a large, half-page notice that said, 'Stop counting. There are 43 photographs in this newspaper.' A few pages later, another large advert read, 'Tell the experimenter you've seen this and win £100' (Wiseman, 2003, pp. 50–51).

So, what happened? A large proportion of the people who considered themselves unlucky flipped right past the adverts. The people who considered themselves lucky were much more likely to see them – and they ended up with the money.

The researchers concluded that people aren't lucky or unlucky, there are just *certain people who are better at noticing, or even creating, chance opportunities.* Their attention is open, and they see more of the world around them. They don't mind adjusting their routine or doing something new; they see things with fresh eyes rather than having selective attention. These individuals end up with a wider range of experiences, meet more people and do more things – and as a result they get more opportunities.

The unlucky people were stuck in routines and didn't notice new chances or opportunities. Their thinking goes a little like this:

Attitude	Emotional response to challenge	Decisions and behaviour	Result
I'm unlucky. Other people seem to get chances and opportunities I don't.	I only have selective attention about chances to try new and interesting things – for example, I don't even see the posters advertising a particular competition. Now it's pretty much the deadline for entries.	I don't bother entering. A fellow student on my course does enter and wins. The first prize is £1,000.	I miss out, and I reinforce my belief that good things only happen to other people. They're lucky and I'm not.

An Experiment

If the research we've described is right, we've all had opportunities and chances to do something new and different, and many of us have missed them.

What might we be missing right now?

Here's an interesting experiment for you to try. In schools and colleges up and down the country, in corridors, receptions, community spaces and classrooms, there are noticeboards. Some of them display student work, some have sports results or calendars, but many of them publicise opportunities.

In this experiment, you're going to wander around the campus and look at twelve different noticeboards. And you're going to *really* notice the things on there – read the flyers, look at the posters, make a note of the clubs, competitions, societies or classes advertised.

Noticeboard	**Location (in case someone else wants to know)**	**Content**
1		
2		
3		
4		
5		
6		
7		
8		

Noticeboard	Location (in case someone else wants to know)	Content
9		
10		
11		
12		

Once you've done this, consider the opportunities available in your organisation. Remember, the lucky people in the experiment simply saw more things in the world around them, and acted on them.

Could you do the same? If you were forced to follow up just one of the leads you've discovered, which one would it be?

36. Attitude Activity: 5, 5, 5

Sometimes study problems can seem insurmountable. And when we're feeling overwhelmed, it's easy to withdraw and let the issues pile up until we feel like we're drowning.

If you've got problems you're trying to solve, you're certainly not alone. This activity is designed to help you get started. It's a simple strategy which asks you to group together your solutions depending on how easy they are to accomplish.

You need to begin with a study problem for this to work, so choose something that's bothering you about the way you approach your studies at the moment. It could be that you find motivation difficult, that you're struggling with a particular topic area or that you keep missing deadlines. Whatever it is, be as specific as possible in defining your issue and make a note of it here:

....

Next, spend some time generating as many solutions to your problem as you can. Don't judge your ideas as they come to you – you won't be doing them all – so feel free to note down everything on paper, from the smallest adjustment or solution to something radical and scary. Aim for at least twenty things you might do to improve your situation. And, remember, anything goes.

....

....

....

....

....

....

....

....

....

Now that you've got a list of actions you could take, use the table below to categorise them according to how easy they would be to implement.

The *five minutes* column is for the solutions that can be actioned quickly – an email, a quick surf of the web, a few minutes finishing a late piece of work.

The *five days* column is for your more ambitious solutions. You could get these done in a working week at school or college if you put your mind to it. They might need two, three or even five steps to complete, but they're doable.

The *five weeks* column is for something that would need a bigger change in behaviour. Five weeks is about the length of a half term, and you only get six of those per year, so it's a solution so radical it will take nearly 20% of a year working on it – a big investment but one you'd be proud of.

Five minutes	**Five days**	**Five weeks**
....	....	....
....	....	....
....	....	....
....	....	....
....	....	....
....	....	....

Hopefully, you should now have a list of possible actions in all three columns.

The ones in the *five minutes* column will be over in the blink of an eye and you can cross them off. Why not choose two of these actions and do them now (right now!).

The *five days* column will be full of potentially interesting solutions. We'd suggest choosing one of these and breaking it down into five short steps. Then make a plan to complete the five steps next week.

1 ....

2 ....

3 ....

4 ....

5 ....

The *five weeks* column may well have some really interesting solutions in it. Some might be ambitious, crazy or almost impossible. Nevertheless, try to choose one – the one you feel you might have a chance of taking some action on.

Take some time over it – just think about what you might need to do if you were to take on one of these more ambitious solutions. How many steps might there be? Can you break it down and just do parts of it? Is there a way to get it started in just five minutes?

Every time you hit obstacles that are getting you down, try this activity. It usually helps to generate solutions and gets students unblocked.

37. Attitude Activity: ODA

Observe, orient, decide, act (OODA) is a famous problem-solving process which was first developed by Colonel John Boyd of the US Air Force in the 1970s. So, can you take these four simple steps whenever you've got an issue with study and, as if by magic, a solution appears?

As you'll know, it's often not that simple. Most study-related problems are really complicated, and a simple four-step approach isn't necessarily helpful. We've found that complex study problems usually involve:

» Habits and beliefs that have strengthened over time and need changing.

» Patterns of behaviour that seem logical but are part of the problem.

» Relationships that aren't straightforward but messy.

» Situations and locations that add to the complexity.

» Resources that are incomplete or missing altogether.

So, how can we make problem-solving a little easier? Over the last few years, inspired by Warren Berger's *The Book of Beautiful Questions* (2019), we've been working with students to develop a problem-solving process that more accurately reflects what it's like to face a problem at school or college.

We've adapted the OODA structure and added a wide array of questions to each part of the process for you to reflect on and consider. The questions should help to unlock solutions, so take your time with them and be ready to make notes.

» **Start with *observe*.** This section requires you to see the problem freshly and clearly, so try not rush through it. Stay here for at least ten minutes; aim for fifteen. You don't have to answer every question, but consider every single one for a moment or two before deciding whether it's useful or not. Make notes as you go – challenge yourself and really get to know your problem from every angle.

» **Now have a go at *decide*.** Stay here for ten minutes, too, checking every question carefully and answering as fully and honestly as possible. Generate as many thoughts and observations as you possibly can, making notes as you go.

- **Finish with *act.*** There's space here to record your plans. You'll have more than one plan – you might have two or three possible solutions that have occurred to you as you answer the questions. Take your time noting them down. Once you've got your solutions, use the remaining questions to test which solution might be best.

Then try it out!

Observe (Why does this problem or situation exist?)
If I had to summarise my problem in one sentence, what would it be?
Why does this problem matter to me?
Why is it happening in the first place?
If I had to blame others for the issue, what would I say?
If I had to take 100% responsibility for the issue, what would I confess to?
Is this a problem that keeps coming back? How have I tried to solve something similar in the past?
Am I really seeing this with fresh eyes or am I repeating old opinions?
What is the evidence behind my beliefs, and how strong is it?
Am I assuming anything without evidence?
What might I be missing?
Do I know another student who has solved this problem already?
Who do I know that's least likely to have this problem? Why?
What am I dreading about this problem? What might I be hiding from?
Does someone else have a totally different reading of this situation?

Decide (What am I really trying to achieve?)
What would a successful outcome look like?
How would I know things were improving? What would I see or feel?
What outcome matters most?
What would a 'good' solution look like?
What have I tried already? Have I been persistent enough in the past?
What character qualities do I have in my favour?
If I could only solve this by stopping doing something, what would it be?
What if I could only take one high-impact action? What would it be?
What would my best teacher advise me to do?
What could I simplify or remove altogether?
What do I keep coming back to as I think?
Who could help me to solve this more quickly?
Act (My shortlist of plans includes ...)
....
....
....
....
....
....
....

Which options are best at allowing me to improve myself?

If I was forced to choose one course of action now, which would it be?

What does my rational self say is the best solution?

Which solutions look the most interesting?

Which might take me furthest fastest?

Which feel like they're quickest to start?

If I could do one thing to make getting started easier, what would it be?

Which solution do I least like? Is it because it will be hard?

If I had to justify a course of action to someone else, what would I say?

38. Attitude Activity: Think Three Positives

Winifred Gallagher is a science writer, magazine editor and journalist. In her 2010 book *Rapt*, she writes about our attention, introducing the idea that we have something she calls 'top-down attention' – that is, attention we decide on and control.

And this top-down attention is like money. We 'pay' attention to things, spending attention like cash during the day. Social media companies want us to 'pay' them – the more people use their sites, the more they can charge for adverts, and the bigger the bonuses for board members. Adverts want our attention. Online apps want it. Emails want it.

But, according to Gallagher, we're in control of where we spend our attention, not them. We can choose what to pay attention to. She goes on to argue that 'deciding what to pay attention to for this hour, day, week, or year … is a predicament, and your quality of life depends on how you handle it. We must resist the temptation to drift along, reacting to whatever happens to us next … and deliberately select targets that are worthy of our finite supplies of time and attention' (Gallagher, 2010, p. 11).

A Week of Positive Things

In this activity, we're going to suggest that you spend one working week – five days – deliberately paying attention to positive things. (Psychologist Martin Seligman has written entire books about how people who focus on positive events, no matter how small, feel much happier, so maybe this will happen to you as well!)

Your aim is to collect three positive things each day.

A couple of rules: (1) you don't need to be winning the lottery – your observation can be very modest, just a small change; and (2) your observation must be specific to that day. Tempting as it is to focus on your family, home or friends, if you're lucky, they're going to be there every day. Instead, you're looking for something that occurred on the day you're thinking about.

Some areas of your life to consider include:

- **Your lessons.** Was there just one moment in a lesson today that was positive? A bad joke, an interesting video, an activity that was OK, an encouraging word from a teacher, a smiley face scribbled in an exercise book, a topic you understood and felt good about?
- **Your interactions.** Was there a connection today that was positive? A friend saying something funny or nice? Someone holding a door open for you? A smile from a teacher or an arm around the shoulder from a friend? A member of the canteen staff saying hello?
- **Your surroundings.** Was there a break in the rain and the sun came out? A warm classroom after a cold break outside? A decent game of netball in the gym or football on the Astroturf? A comfy chair in a common room or study space?
- **Your journeys.** Was there a moment on the bus that brightened your day? A chat while you walked between lessons? A discussion in the lunch queue or a walk with a friend?

For each day, record the three things. We bet that you're feeling more positive about your studies by the end of the week!

39. Attitude Activity: The Myth of the Curve

You'll have heard the phrase 'learning curve'. It describes the process of getting better at something. Sometimes, when a task is challenging, we use the phrase 'steep learning curve' to describe how hard it will be.

But we think there's a problem with the word 'curve'. It suggests the process will be smooth, and in our experience, learning is almost never smooth. There are setbacks, plateaus and sudden jumps forward – less like a neat curve and much more like a series of rising hills.

There really are periods of time when progress flattens out. We call these 'progress plateaus'. These are the times when you're making hard-won changes to the way you work, but they don't seem to be producing any difference in performance. Like these frustrating examples:

» You're working way harder than you were, but there's no change in your grades – yet.

» You've got to grips with getting up early, so your attendance and punctuality have improved, but no one seems to have noticed.

» You're revising differently, pushing yourself to do more challenging work, but your test results haven't changed that much.

There are tons of other examples of study changes taking a while to have an impact. And what is it tempting to do while we wait for that impact to emerge? Jump to a hasty conclusion: 'What's the point? I tried it for a little while but it made no difference. Waste of energy. I may as well go back to doing things the way I was.'

Before you do, try this activity. We've found it's a great one to help you persevere when your momentum seems to vanish. It's about changing the way you measure progress. Progress isn't just test scores or grades; although these are nice to have, they often take longer to arrive. Progress starts as micro-changes in other measurements. Consider the following and note down some thoughts.

Progress in peace of mind	Progress in confidence	Progress in time management
You're feeling better about your study habits. You're worrying less or feeling less stressed; you feel optimistic for the first time in ages; you're conquering unhelpful habits; you're enjoying classes more.	You're feeling on top of your classes. You can follow complex discussions more easily; you find yourself answering difficult questions quite well; you understand something a classmate doesn't.	You're getting to grips with tasks as you rebalance. You have a clear sense of what you've got to do; you don't wake at night in a cold sweat; you feel in control of your time; you don't forget things and schedule work better.
....	....	....

Capturing examples of these micro-changes in well-being, confidence or study management helps to remind you that you are moving forward. These improvements in the way you feel are worth the work. And, soon enough, they'll be followed by upward movement in grades too. You just have to stick at it.

40. Attitude Activity: Worst-Case Scenarios

This activity was inspired by the work of writer and entrepreneur Tim Ferriss who openly admits that, like many of us, he feels the pressure when there's a lot on the line. The activity that follows is based on a process suggested by Ferriss in his 2017 TED talk, in which he discusses something he calls 'fear-setting' – a process that can help us all to tackle and tame our fears.

The thinking behind the activity is this: many of us write down our goals (we often talk of 'goal setting') and record plans for achieving them, but we rarely record our fears. Instead, our fears stay in our minds, where they get distorted and exaggerated. We carry them around with us every day, creating worst-case scenarios and fretting constantly, imagining what if …

» We fail an important test, exam or portfolio submission.

» We drop a grade and can't get into our first-choice university or college.

» We can't motivate ourselves and end up doing no work between now and the end of term.

» We have to listen to teachers making critical comments at parents' evening.

Rather than carrying our fears around every day, suffering as we imagine them all coming true, we could instead get them out of our heads and onto paper. That way, we can put our worst-case scenarios under a microscope and study them objectively. We've adapted Ferriss' method to suit an educational context and given you an example to guide you. Here's what to do:

1 First, *define* your worst-case scenario. Write it down objectively without using emotional language; just a statement of fact at the top of the table below (e.g. 'I miss the grades needed for my chosen degree course,' not 'My grades are terrible and everything's a disaster').

2 Underneath, in the *prevent* column, record all the things you could do to either prevent or lower the likelihood of the fear coming true. Keep your actions small and realistic.

3 In the *repair* column, list all the actions you could take to fix things if the worst-case scenario happened. Again, keep them realistic and achievable.

4 Finally, in the *upside* column, record the potentially good things that might happen as a result of your worst-case scenario coming true: lessons you learn, skills you develop, relationships that are strengthened, new opportunities that might arise.

Check out our example:

Define: **I get a C in biology, miss my offer and get rejected from Bristol University.**		
Prevent: I could take the following achievable actions to lower the likelihood of my worst-case scenario coming true.	**Repair:** If my worst-case scenario happened, I could take the following actions to try and partially fix things.	**Upside:** The potential positives that might arise if my worst-case scenario happened are:
I could meet with another student who's really good at the bits of the course I can't do. **I could ask my teacher for a one-to-one on the hard sections of the course.** **I could make small adjustments to my revision to give me more time on biology.** **I could do more past papers, focusing on the hard questions.**	**I could contact the university and ask to be reconsidered if a student with an offer decides not to take it up.** **I could go through clearing.** **I could start a closely related course, then ask to be transferred onto biology after the first year.** **I could start a similar course with a slightly lower entry requirement.**	**I might end up at another university and really enjoy the course.** **I might end up much more resilient because I've worked harder and solved problems.** **I might meet a really inspiring professor at another university.** **My experience might mean I'm well-placed to help others.**

Now it's your turn:

Define:		
Prevent: I could take the following achievable actions to lower the likelihood of my worst-case scenario coming true.	**Repair:** If my worst-case scenario happened, I could take the following actions to try and partially fix things.	**Upside:** The potential positives that might arise if my worst-case scenario happened are:
....	....	....
....	....	....
....	....	....
....	....	....
....	....	....
....	....	....
....	....	....

Hopefully, this activity will help you to get a clearer sense of perspective when everything feels overwhelming.

It pays back the time you put into it by calming your mind and giving you a better quality of life. Try it – what's the worst that could happen?

6. Curriculum

Let's take a minute. You might have just skimmed through forty possible activities, mentally selecting the ones that look like they might work for your students. As a result, you might be feeling overwhelmed: how on earth do we go from glancing through the material to delivering it in real life?

Being teachers, we're used to anticipating and managing practicalities, and if you're anything like us, that's where your mind might leap next. Who delivers this? What about that grumpy staff member who's going to hate it? How do the students respond to activities and record their thoughts? What if the students don't like it? Even if we wanted to try it, where would we fit it in?

We've written about implementation before in *The A Level Mindset* (Chapter 7: Making it Happen) and *The GCSE Mindset* (Chapter 13: Implementation), and we don't want to repeat ourselves here. Instead, we're going to briefly summarise our approaches in five principles.

1. Start small and control the controllables

If you've got a choice of beginning your VESPA project with a whole school or just one key stage, choose the key stage. If you've got a choice of starting it with a whole key stage or a single year within that key stage, choose the latter. If you've got the choice of beginning it with an entire year or two tutor groups within that year, go for the two small groups. And if you've got an opportunity to try it yourself alongside two keen colleagues, scoping it out with no pressure – well, you get the idea. Educating is hard enough as it is. Stack the deck in your favour.

2. Build a coalition of the willing

Although our practical minds might seek symmetry and consistency – every student needs to be doing this at the same time or it's not fair – we've found that projects develop best when a small willing group work together first. Build a working party. Find the staff who are interested. Introduce the ideas in a meeting and move forward experimentally, trying some of the activities and feeding back to each other. If you're a head of year considering how these materials might benefit your Year 11s, could you use some activities in assembly and find two tutors who are excited by the project to run others with their groups? The same goes for students; if you're considering a cohort of students who aren't hitting their target grades, work with the individuals who seem as if they want to change first. Is there a group eager to be doing better? A cohort that isn't where they want to be and aspire to improve? If you ran voluntary drop-in sessions, who would turn up? If you asked the attendees to recommend a friend to come along, who might show up next? Are there alumni who might advocate for certain activities and deliver them for you?

3. Run a short-term research project

Choose a cohort of students and collect some baseline data before you begin: a questionnaire summarising their study skills, their attendance, their opinions about the support they get, their mock exam grades – whatever works for you. Then run a six-week VESPA research project. At the end, ask the same questions again, allowing the students to give you written feedback too, and see if you've moved the needle. As you present your findings to others, bear this in mind: other staff are often persuaded in different ways. Some want to see data: 'Is there any evidence that this works?' Others want to hear case studies of individuals and connect with those students. Others enjoy the camaraderie and togetherness of the job, and want confirmation that a project involves engaging teamwork and feelings of success.

As you're putting together the results of your project, begin with the data. Over the years, we've measured the number of students choosing to study independently in a school library, and seen it go up as we used VESPA activities about focus and flow (try Activity 12: Disruption Cost and Deep Work). Or we've asked students to declare the levels of effort they're putting into their studies at the start and end of a research project, and seen it go up significantly. Or we gather qualitative data – are students feeling more satisfied with the support they're getting? Once you've covered the data, placate the staff who respond to individual stories of success by including student quotes and case studies. Finish by emphasising the professional satisfaction of the teachers who took part. If you present your findings in this way, you'll find you have others who want to give it a try too.

4. Co-design curricula

The curriculum examples we give below are a good starting point, but there's nothing to stop you working with a group of staff to choose their favourites. Take the forty we've suggested and select the twenty you prefer. Then give a team of staff permission to choose their favourite ten from that twenty. These become your 'core' curriculum; the rest you can save for interventions and coaching conversations.

5. Move in phases

Imagine larger scale change happening in phases. Phase one involves the early adopters. Envisage departments with a settled roster of staff and an established head who are ready to deliver something new, or tutor groups that are expertly led and enjoying a positive culture created by an inspirational leader. Phase one is about staff who are hungry to have a go. It might last a term or a full year, and it ends with a sharing of expertise. Phase two might be teams or departments who come on board once this initial scoping out has happened. Each phase two leader might have a phase one mentor. This phase might last another term or a full year. Phases three and four see the project out to its conclusion.

You don't need to torture yourself imagining all your plans collapsing at the hands of a small number of disengaged staff; they're your phase four or five cohort – and you'll have much greater momentum by then. In short: first, ensure the project is robust in your context; figure out which sessions are likely to have the impact you want to create a curriculum that is perfect for your students and their specific challenges; then roll it out to larger numbers.

Whatever you decide to try first, staff often want a centrally delivered curriculum that anticipates and responds to the challenges of the academic year. We've got several suggestions for you to browse here, so let's consider a few.

Six-Week Experiments

Rather than make a huge commitment to training a tutor team, launching the VESPA concept and co-designing a year-long curriculum, one way forward with your project might be to try a series of mini curricula with targeted cohorts.

We've made two suggestions here. Both will work perfectly well, but think of them as a starting point for your own bespoke six-week project. We try to consider half terms as six or seven week-long periods dominated by particular themes and challenges, so the curriculum you select for half term two (October to Christmas) might focus on keeping up levels of energy and positivity as the nights draw in, whereas the one you need for half term four (February to Easter) might use the approaching break as a focal point for a series of tasks about systems or practice.

An exam-preparation curriculum for a year group approaching the end of a key stage

In this example, we've sequenced six activities around effort and practice that we hope might encourage some reflection and planning in the six-week half term before the Easter holidays. What we're aiming for here is accelerating the movement from preparation-phase revision (copying out notes, rereading textbooks, highlighting key terms) towards performance-phase revision (high-utility strategies, active recall, testing) by exploring and discussing some of the differences in the weeks running up to the break and frameworking a few revision sessions to minimise anxiety. What we're trying to avoid is the prospect of students spending seventeen days away from school either swerving revision entirely because of the fear of starting or spending hours on low-utility copying and rereading when they could have begun the process earlier.

You might look at our choice of activities and feel they could be adjusted or improved, or indeed augmented by activities from *The A Level Mindset* (Activity 29: Two Slow, One Fast would work well in this context) or *The GCSE Mindset* (Activity 34: Finding Flow would fit nicely here too.) That's fine – go ahead and experiment.

Week 1	Week 2	Week 3	Week 4	Week 5	Week 6
Discussion: What makes a successful student? What do we need to achieve over the coming half term?	**Activity 14: Activating and Sustaining** A discussion of motivational techniques – and a plan to try new ones.	**Activity 25: High and Low Utility** A first look at the idea of utility, involving discussion and reflection.	**Activity 29: Cog P versus Cog A** Plan a cognitively active revision session and feed back once it's done.	**Activity 26: Closed Book Note-Taking** Revise a topic using a from-memory study technique.	**Activity 27: Verbal Recaps** Plan a revision session where you teach an imaginary class using the script.

A transition curriculum – standard-setting for a new key stage

In this curriculum, we're imagining six weeks in which we establish how study will be different this year. It might work nicely, therefore, with a group of Year 10s or Year 12s beginning their GCSE or A level journeys in half term one (September to October). We're aiming to provide some clarity around expectations so the students know what higher levels of effort look like; an opportunity for them to outline some goals for the year or years ahead; and a tactic that helps them to cope effectively when resources begin to pile up and new and challenging deadlines loom. So, we've got a mixture of vision, systems and effort here. Again, you might want to consider this in terms of your own context and decide how it needs to be different. Working with staff teaching retake GCSE courses in further education contexts, for example, we were struck by how they wanted to prioritise attitude in the opening sections of their courses – a fact that seems obvious in retrospect.

Week 1	Week 2	Week 3	Week 4	Week 5	Week 6
Discussion: What makes a successful student? What habits and approaches might we need to tackle this higher level of learning?	**Activity 5: Outcome Control** Do our goals respond to the amount of control we have over the outcome? Should we be specific or general? Reflection followed by goal setting.	**Activity 19: Pending, Doing, Done** What are our to-do lists looking like? How to prioritise and focus.	**Activity 9: Proactive versus Reactive** Plan a week of proactive study activities.	**Activity 10: The Peloton** A chance to consider our performance relative to others and to think about positioning. What does a good position look like?	**Activity 16: Red Flag Rescue Plans** Are we maintaining a good start or slacking off? Plan for self-intervention if effort drops.

Short curricula like this give you a chance to sample some of the sessions and begin to learn how to best deliver them in your context. You might find that, on reflection, you need Activity 6: Twenty-Five Minute Sprints from *The GCSE Mindset* here, or you might want to make space for Activity 9: The 1–10 Scale from *The A Level Mindset*.

The staff and students involved might choose their 'most impactful activity' at the end; a group of students keen on developing their leadership and presentation skills might advocate for a particular activity and go and teach it to your Year 10s during form period; another group might visit the senior leadership team and present a short summary of the kind of work they've been doing. There might be a presentation to parents, a short video summarising some of the student feedback or a piece of action research that uses the VESPA questionnaire to measure impact (see Chapter 7) or reflect on the mock or exam grades the cohort achieved compared to a control group.

Twelve-Week Experiments

If you're feeling more confident, but still want a project you can get your arms around and control, a term-long, twelve-week curriculum might be the answer. The example we're going to suggest runs in term two of the academic year. We're offering up this middle term as an example partly because we want to demonstrate how schools and colleges needn't begin in September or consider the opportunity entirely missed, and partly because mid-year starts often work well as a sense of frustration around learners' levels of proactivity and independence has usually surfaced by this point, and one of the drivers of change is often this sense of dissatisfaction. As a leader, you can use it to kick-start the planning of a new way of approaching the problem.

There's another advantage to the term-long curriculum running in the spring; you have time to plan it carefully in the autumn and to reflect on your successes and setbacks as you pick over the project in the summer. It's this process of feedback, assessment and discussion that generates a stronger curriculum the following year; staff get to throw out sessions they feel didn't go well, lobby for more sessions about particular elements of the model, share approaches and pick out cohorts of students who need additional support.

In the example below, we've chosen to begin with vision – we'd be running the first session in January, after all, and surely we can't pass up the new year as an opportunity to discuss hopes for the future. We've also pushed pretty hard on effort, knowing as we do that January and February can be tough months for sustaining engagement. As we head towards the second half of the term, you can see our focus shift towards practice, as we encourage students out of the passive collection and curation of neat learning materials towards greater levels of challenge. And we're also foregrounding attitude in this curriculum, with a focus on problem-solving and resilient optimism. Once again, feel free to adjust this depending on the needs of your students.

Week 1	Week 2	Week 3	Week 4	Week 5	Week 6
Discussion: What makes a successful student? What habits and approaches might we need this coming term and year?	**Activity 1: Diver Goals and Thriver Goals** An investigation into types of goals and having a sense of purpose. What might our thriver goals be?	**Activity 4: A Question of Money** What does a great job look like? What characteristics might we be looking for? Discussion and reflection.	**Break:** Reflection and planning, file checks or coaching conversations, catching up and looking ahead.	**Activity 37: ODA** All of us have study problems – it's how we deal with them that counts. A chance to work through a problem.	**Activity 13: Questify** Can we tackle an epic piece of work in the run-up to the break, then finish it over half term? Making plans for catching up.
Week 8	**Week 9**	**Week 10**	**Week 11**	**Week 12**	**Week 13**
Activity 33: NAF and NACH Can we develop our attitudes to challenge over the coming half term?	**Activity 18: Night School** Designing a system for study at home that promotes time and attention management.	**Activity 29: Cog P versus Cog A** Plan a cognitively active revision or study session and feed back once it's done.	**Break:** Reflection and planning, file checks or coaching conversations, catching up and looking ahead.	**Activity 28: Test Your Future Self** How often do we actively test our recall? A quick method for boosting how much we can recall.	**Activity 34: Check Ahead, Check Back** How are we doing relative to others? Can we check back and assess what we're proud of?

An activity a week might feel like the right kind of pace in your context, and that's fine, but here you'll see that we've aimed to occasionally build in space for reflection and planning, catching up or looking ahead. We find these pockets of time really valuable. Students might grab the chance to do something as simple as tidy their notes, glue in stray handouts and check the deadlines they have coming up. Or you might ask them to think about the last few activities and pick one that's had some sort of impact on their thinking – they might not have taken action yet, but thinking is a good start. You might film short twenty-second responses to a question like, 'If I was starting the year again, what would I do differently?' to create a resource for next year's students. (We've also asked our learners to write messages to future students, outlining three pieces of advice. It's always nice to hand out those letters in a tutorial session months later.) Consider The Motivation Diamond (Activity 1 in *The GCSE Mindset*) as part of this twelve-week curriculum or explore one of our favourites – Getting Dreams Done (Activity 2 in *The A Level Mindset*).

The Year-Long Curriculum: Core Curriculum and Coaching Curriculum

You'll notice a slowing down of the pace in the model that follows. We're suggesting leading an activity every two weeks here, giving students time to let these new approaches bed in. We're sacrificing volume of material for what we hope will become deeper thinking and greater reflection. (The sessions could easily be supported through assemblies in the alternate weeks or discussion sessions similar to the breaks suggested in the curriculum above.)

What we're proposing is a *core curriculum* of eighteen activities that all students get to hear about and explore, represented in the plans below. For this particular curriculum, we've assumed that some sort of testing comes in the summer term, so we've built up to that and left some space for the test period. Remember, these are entirely adjustable and just a starting point for your planning.

This core is then supplemented by a *coaching curriculum* of twenty-two activities (basically, whatever is left over) that staff can use with cohorts of students, safe in the knowledge that the activities won't have been explored in a tutorial period. The coaching curriculum might resource a conversation, help to structure a chance discussion with a group of distracted students or provide an activity for a small cohort of students gathered together following their responses to the VESPA questionnaire.

Term 1 (seven activities)

Week 1	Week 2	Week 3	Week 4	Week 5	Week 6
Discussion: What makes a successful student? What habits and approaches might we need this coming year?	**Activity 5: Outcome Control** Do our goals respond to the amount of control we have over the outcome? Should we be specific or general? Reflection followed by goal setting.	**Activity 23: Cornell Notes** Does the way we take notes impact on our performance? Experiments in new ways of note-taking.		**Activity 15: The Clarity Countdown** An approach to study that avoids compounding mistakes. Do we clear up potential errors quickly? Which subjects could benefit from this approach?	
Week 8	**Week 9**	**Week 10**	**Week 11**	**Week 12**	**Week 13**
Activity 9: Proactive versus Reactive Plan a week of proactive study activities.		**Activity 19: Pending, Doing, Done** What are our to-do lists looking like? How to prioritise and focus.	**Activity 24: 1% Planning** No matter how overwhelmed we feel, we can always focus on the next action.		**Activity 34: Check Ahead, Check Back** The term draws to a close! Can we check back and assess what we're proud of?

Term 2 (six activities and a revisit)

Week 1	Week 2	Week 3	Week 4	Week 5	Week 6
Activity 1: Diver Goals and Thriver Goals An investigation into types of goals and having a sense of purpose. What might our thriver goals be?		**Activity 5: Outcome Control** Do our goals respond to the amount of control we have over the outcome? Should we be specific or general?		**Revisit: Proactive versus Reactive** Plan another week of proactive study activities.	
Week 8	**Week 9**	**Week 10**	**Week 11**	**Week 12**	**Week 13**
Activity 22: Have To, Ought To, Want To How balanced are our weeks? Have we lost touch with clubs, sports, hobbies and exciting projects?		**Activity 36: 5, 5, 5** A first look at the idea of analytical problem-solving, involving honest discussion and planning.		**Activity 29: Cog P versus Cog A** An introduction to revision, with a focus on active study methods.	**Activity 39: The Myth of the Curve** The term draws to a close! A good time to assess the progress we're making, even if it's not yet evidenced in grades.

Term 3 (five activities)

Week 1	Week 2	Week 3	Week 4	Week 5	Week 6
Activity 25: High and Low Utility A deeper exploration of the idea of utility, involving discussion and reflection.		**Activity 28: Test Your Future Self** Practice tests have the highest impact on our performance – and we can learn to set our own tests!		**Activity 27: Verbal Recaps** Plan a revision session where you teach an imaginary class using scripts.	**Activity 11: Becoming Indistractable** Designing routines and spaces that take us through the period of testing coming up.
Week 8	**Week 9**	**Week 10**	**Week 11**	**Week 12**	**Week 13**
			Activity 2: Sweet and Sour Summers Imagining a summer holiday in which we get to shadow certain jobs. What might those jobs be?		

One of the key things to remember when designing curricula like these is to do it alongside the school or college calendar. We want students to hear the right messages, but we also want them to hear the right messages at the best possible time. You have everything you need here in this book, but there are eighty more activities in the other two. An upcoming parents' evening might get you thinking about whether you need to include The Roadmap (Activity 5 in *The GCSE Mindset*), or a particularly tricky period of submissions in BTEC subjects might have you considering whether The Energy Line (Activity 7 in *The A Level Mindset*) might be a timely addition to your curriculum.

Delivering Activities

At the conclusion to this section is a delivery script you might find useful, but before you check it out, it's important to note that we've developed it to help staff get a sense of the tone and tenor of the sessions, not as a means of specifying word-for-word delivery.

What we want to emphasise through the script is the difference between a VESPA session and a lesson. When we're delivering one of these activities, we're not just imparting information and instructions; we're running a workshop or structured discussion during which learners get to experiment with a new way of doing something.

We're not urging the replacement of their current approaches – 'You must all stop doing it the old way; here's the new way.' Instead, we're looking to engage students, getting them to reflect on the ways in which they currently work and investigate new or different ways to solve a study-related problem.

As such, many of the methods we might use to measure the success of a conventional lesson (Can the students accurately recall what we've covered? Have they retained the information, listened to feedback and adjusted their behaviour as a result?) might not apply immediately, or at all. Instead, we might observe smaller changes in student behaviour over time.

Stage one, as we cover the first two or three activities, might be a growing awareness that ability doesn't equal outcome, that a range of non-cognitive factors play an important role in success. We might not see this immediately. Stay positive and patient.

Stage two, as we progress through the first five or six activities, might involve a critical assessment of current performance; the students might be privately asking themselves questions like, 'What is my effort like? Am I organised enough? Do I revise in the right way?' We're surfacing habits of thought and building self-awareness. This stage isn't always comfortable for students; we're pushing them to realise that they might need to work differently, after all.

Stage three might be the response we hope for straight away but in fact takes a little longer to come. Here, we see an openness to change and a willingness to experiment with the suggested tools, engage in discussion and feedback, and adjust work patterns.

So, we need positive patience as we present the materials. It's that tone of persistent, engaged and eager exploration of new and better ways of working that we're trying to capture in the scripts.

We've gone for a simple four-part structure: the introduction, the anecdote, the activity and the reflection.

The *introduction* is your chance to engage students, to make a pitch for what we're doing today and why:

> **Today we're going to spend a little time exploring a new study technique. It's my job to give you all the support you need to become a better learner – but to challenge you sometimes too. I wouldn't be doing my job properly if I didn't share this with you. It might not be for everyone, but give it a go and let's see what you think …**

The *anecdote* gives you the chance to tie the activity to a real-life context, case or circumstance which strengthens your case for sharing the activity. We've given you three suggestions here:

> ***A personal story:*** **So, before we dive in, let's set the scene. I'm going to tell you about a challenge I faced at university. It was my second year, and I completely lost my motivation. I remember feeling …**
>
> ***A story about another (anonymous) student:*** **Before we start, I want to tell you a little bit about a student who was sitting right where you are a couple of years ago. He always used to struggle with revision, and one day …**
>
> ***A story from another source:*** **Before we begin, let's start by looking at this video/article/advert/headline/study …**

Then you're into the *activity* itself:

> **So, that's why we're doing this today – and it's perfect for this time of year. Now, you might not feel this applies to you now, and that's fine, but at some point in the future, this approach/tactic might be a real lifesaver.**

Finally, in the closing minutes of a session, it's time for the *reflection*:

> **What do you think? Are you likely to give this a go in the future? Has it made you change your thinking in any way? Was it at all useful?**
>
> *And, if not:* **Has anyone got a better way of tackling the problem?**
>
> *Or:* **If this one's not for you, that's fine. What other tricks, tactics or techniques might we consider?**

Remember, you needn't feel threatened by students telling you, 'This one isn't useful for me.' We're all different. 'No problem,' you can say, 'there's another one along next week, and you might find that one helpful.' But do push the student to offer an alternative course of action. We're not about allowing complete disengagement here. We're encouraging critical reflection and – as the case may be – rejection of the tool only following experimentation and consideration.

Encourage the student to tell you why. 'Is there a particular reason this doesn't click with you?' Then, push for another possibility. 'OK. Talk me through how you do things at the moment. If there's a better way of doing this, I'd love to hear all about it.' In this way, we can establish whether the rejection comes after reflection or if it's a knee-jerk reaction to being challenged.

Students have reported that the questionnaires and activities have helped them to identify and make real changes to their current approach. It has helped to move students from 'knowing' to 'doing' change.

7. Introducing the VESPA Psychometric Questionnaire

In 2016, we worked closely with Dr Neil Dagnall and Dr Andrew Denovan, psychologists at Manchester Metropolitan University, to develop a psychometric questionnaire that would measure students' levels of vision, effort, systems, practice and attitude.

Our experts' domain knowledge and insight was hugely impressive. They were invaluable in developing and testing a list of twenty-eight questions, delivered in the form of statements with a Likert scale, to create a student profile – a score out of ten for each element of the model.

Building a questionnaire like this involved a complex and rigorous process. Dagnall and Denovan began by trialling the twenty-eight statements with 1,669 students to ensure what they call its 'internal reliability' (its stability – the likelihood that the statements mean the same thing to everyone who responds, that they might produce the same results and that each statement is reliably connected to the characteristic it's measuring).

Internal reliability in psychometric tests can be gauged in several ways. It's often measured by something statisticians call Cronbach's alpha, a measure named after educational psychologist and Stanford professor Lee Cronbach, first proposed in 1951. The measure gives a score between zero and one; the closer to one a score is, the more internally reliable a measurement is, with one being a 'perfect' measurement of something. Agreement about what constitutes a 'good' score is often debated, as you might expect, but 0.7 is considered sufficient for early stage research and 0.8 for applied research. The VESPA questionnaire scores 0.85.

It scores similarly well when put through other measures of reliability. Dagnall and Denovan ran an advanced statistical analysis procedure known as 'confirmatory factor analysis', which measures the robustness of the link between the proxy (i.e. the questionnaire statement) and its relationship to the concept (i.e. vision, effort and so on). Without going into complex and confusing detail, the questionnaire scores within the statistically acceptable boundaries for all the elements measured, including – and to us non-statisticians, these terms will mean nothing – the comparative fit index, incremental fit index, root mean square error of approximation and standard root mean square residual. Our experts even went as far as checking each question separately to see how strongly each 'loads' onto its respective factor. 'Overall,' Dagnall and Denovan (2017, p. 218) conclude, 'these results suggest that the twenty-eight item VESPA can be considered an internally reliable measure.'

How Can the Questionnaire Be Useful for You?

There is a copy of the questionnaire's twenty-eight items in *The GCSE Mindset* (p. 218), but an online version was created in 2018 by Tony Dennis, whose VESPA expertise was developed while working as a head of sixth form.*

The online version has several impressive advantages. One of Dennis' most powerful additions has been the ability to benchmark scores for each component – a process that first began with a study of two thousand students from across the UK and from a range of educational contexts. The results were analysed and used to transpose the original five-point Likert scale into a ten-point student score for each component. (This process is now repeated annually to ensure our benchmark scores are as accurate as we can make them. We're aiming to provide confidence that the student scores are relative to the thousands of other students undertaking the VESPA psychometric questionnaire from across the world each year.)

The size of the operation means the collected data becomes gradually more and more robust. At the time of writing, over thirty thousand students from across the world are using VESPA reports to identify key metacognitive aspects of their study and improve their chances of academic success. These are learners from a wide range of countries and contexts; there are grammar schools, comprehensives, private schools, sixth-form colleges, further education colleges, universities, specialist post-16 providers and hospital schools from as far apart as Peru, Portugal, Qatar, Italy, the Cayman Islands and Thailand.

Operating online has had other advantages: it means students can gain instant feedback following completion of the questionnaire; automated and bespoke reports are generated immediately for both students and staff. We've worked on the reports for years now to ensure that they provide detailed feedback, coaching questions and a tailored selection of VESPA activities based on the score profile of the student.

And one final note on the data collected: our online programme – the psychometric and associated reports – is registered with the Information Commissioner's Office, the UK's independent body set up to uphold information rights, and we maintain the highest standards of data protection, only collecting the information essential to generating and sharing the questionnaire results. We never collect personal data, we don't share data with any third parties and all

* It's available at www.vespa.academy/portal.html.

data is protected using the highest levels of encryption. When results of the questionnaire are used for research purposes, we obtain written permission from the school or organisation, and fully anonymise the data.

The Reports

Very simply, the online psychometric questionnaire produces clear, striking and helpful visual summaries of the data collected, allowing users to quickly analyse and identify new insights and areas for intervention. Take a typical overview report, for example, which allows users to see instantly how a large cohort of students are scoring themselves. Here's an example of a set of C1 results (C1 means cycle 1 – students can take the questionnaire up to three times in an academic year):

What we're seeing here is a quick surface sense of where the cohort are currently, and – from the smaller number below the main score – an awareness of where the cohort might be relative to the thousands of other students who've completed the questionnaire in that year. The data is interactive; by hovering and clicking, users can dive into a score for vision, for example, and then sort every student response from highest to lowest, or draw up lists of students who scored themselves 'lower than 3' or 'higher than 7'.

Now, consider this set of C1 vision scores reproduced, with kind permission, from Neath and Port Talbot College:

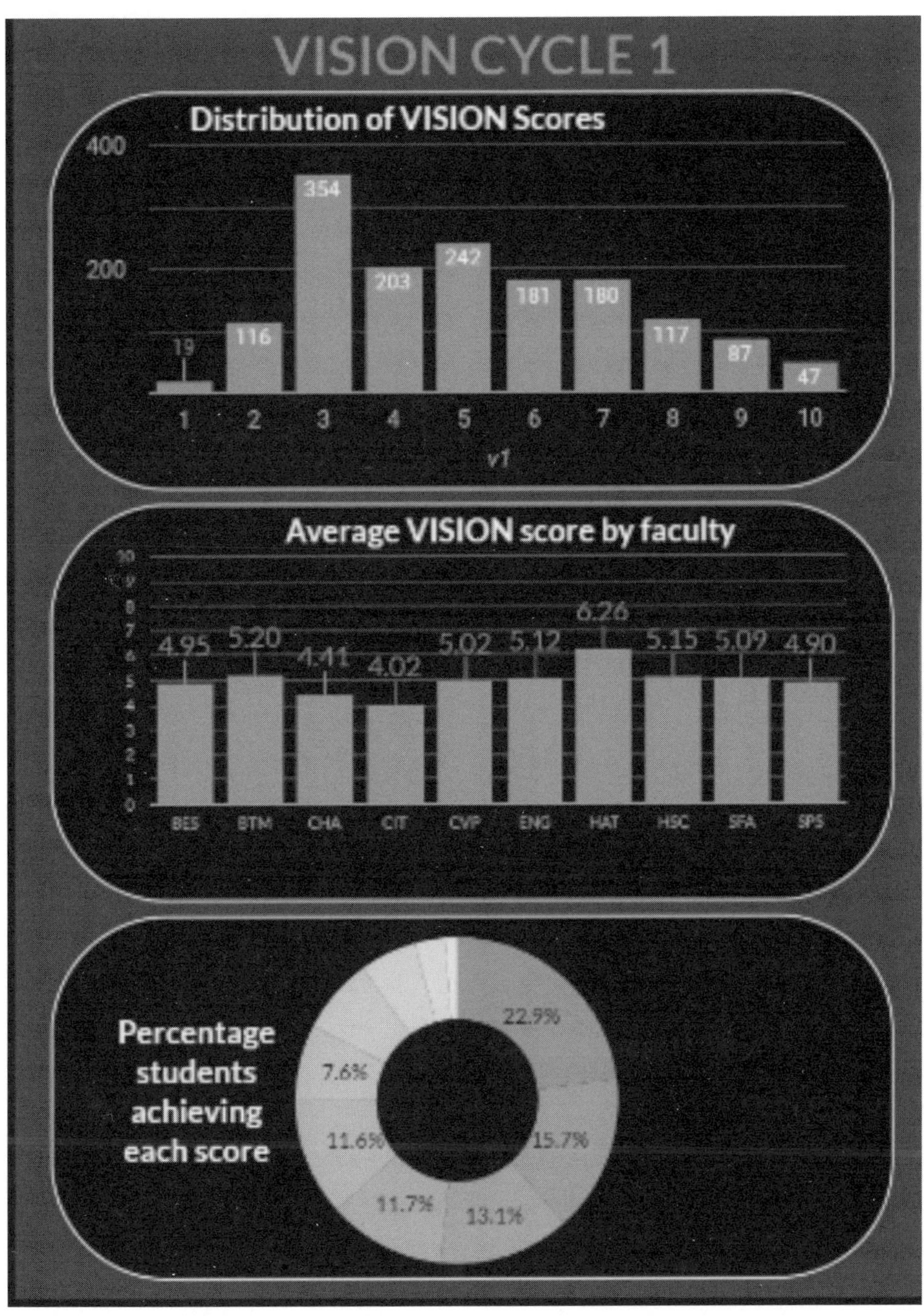

What we have here is a chance to explore cohorts in much more detail. For each element of the model, we can use data like this to click on each column and bring up the names of each student represented, the individual faculties involved or the nineteen learners who've scored themselves '1' for vision, for example.

Remember, this kind of self-reporting is only the starting point for a discussion. You might encounter a student who says, 'My score is wrong.' If that's the case – it happens once every ten times or so – it isn't something we need to panic about. We can simply ask, 'OK. What score do you think you deserve for vision? Can you explain a little about why you think that score is more appropriate?' One of the great strengths of the VESPA questionnaire is as a tool for starting and frameworking useful conversations.

The student report looks a little different. Here's an example:

LEVEL 3 VESPA STUDENT REPORT

FULL NAME	CYCLE	GROUP	DATE & TIME COMPLETED

VISION SCORE - YOU KNOW WHAT YOU WANT TO ACHIEVE AND WHY

1	2	3	4	5	6	7	8	9	10

You are a person with a reasonably clear idea of what you want to do in the future, but you might not be 100% sure whether university, employment or work-based training is the right choice for you. You might have two or three options that you spend lots of time comparing. Generally, when you set goals you are committed to them, although you might sometimes find yourself distracted or changing your mind. You generally finish projects that you start. You may need to narrow down your options and work on a more specific action plan.

Key Questions: What job would you do for free? Have you spoken to a careers advisor? Have you written down your goals?
Suggested Vision Tools: Perfect Day, Fix your Dashboard, Fake it

EFFORT SCORE - YOU PUT IN THE REQUIRED HOURS OF INDEPENDENT WORK

1	2	3	4	5	6	7	8	9	10

You are a reasonably hard-working student, but you know that you could be working harder. You generally use your study periods effectively and complete tasks to a good level. On occasion, you may cut corners or rush tasks. You work hard in most classes, but perhaps you could be more actively involved in class; though you might set yourself extra work now and again it's not something you do regularly. How could you improve your effort habit? Are there particular subjects where you could increase your effort?

Key Questions: Do you think you are working hard enough? Who do you sit next to in classes? Do they work the same way as you?
Suggested Effort Tools: The 1-10 Scale, Inner Storytelling, The 3 R's of Habit

SYSTEMS SCORE - YOU ARE ORGANISED

1	2	3	4	5	6	7	8	9	10

This systems score suggests you are fairly good at organising your time, and sometimes meet deadlines. However, it also suggests you don't always complete your homework on time, particularly in busy weeks. You can make good study notes but are also a bit disorganised and inconsistent. Your files and folders might benefit from an overhaul – you might know deep down there are things likely to be missing and forgotten. How are you currently organising your week? Could you create a better system to help you organise your time and resources?

Key Questions: Do you use a planner or diary to record tasks? Could you create a better system to help you organise your time and resources?
Suggested Systems Tools: The Energy Line, The Breakfast Club, Snack don't Binge

PRACTICE SCORE - YOU USE A VARIETY OF REVISION TECHNIQUES

1	2	3	4	5	6	7	8	9	10

You use a reasonable range of revision strategies such as completing past paper questions under timed conditions. You might have handed in extra work for marking or sought feedback on how you can improve but you might not be as consistent as you want. You know you should be setting yourself challenging revision tasks, and often you do so. Other times, you might find yourself just re-reading notes or highlighting. Do you revise as efficiently as you could? When completing past paper questions do you always practice under timed conditions?

Key Questions: What do you do with the feedback you get on marked work? If you do past paper questions - do you mark them?
Suggested Practice Tools: The Revision Questionnaire, Learn from your mistakes, The Leitner Box

ATTITUDE SCORE - YOU BOUNCE BACK FROM SETBACKS

1	2	3	4	5	6	7	8	9	10

You often feel confident and in control before tests and exams. You also feel confident in your own abilities, though there are infrequent occasions where you might question yourself. You recognise the importance of hard work and practice, and believe your effort will pay off. You can handle a challenging lesson or two without feeling insecure and you can cope well with setbacks, unless a number arrive all at once. You might be shielding yourself from some challenges, though. What lessons could you learn from your failures?

Key Questions: What's the best feedback you've had this term?What techniques do you use to stay calm?
Suggested Attitude Tools: Force Field Analysis, Falling Forwards, Kill your Critic

OVERALL VESPA SCORE

You currently have a VESPA score which suggests you are generally independent, capable and organised. It's likely that you aren't quite as consistent as you would like, with some weaker areas among your evident strengths. You are pretty clear on why you are studying, and you handle the pressure of study well. However, your mindset isn't set forever and changes as you move through life. So how can you continue to develop your VESPA score? Which areas could you improve in?

We often conduct coaching conversations following the completion of the questionnaire, beginning by asking students how accurate they think the report is and why. A brief response in prose often helps them to organise their thoughts, so you might ask them to reflect on the report and write two short paragraphs, the first outlining the accuracy of the report and the second summarising what they think they need to work on.

Notice the 'key questions' generated by the report. We've worked on these carefully to ensure they're thought-provoking and interesting, and as such they might be a good place to begin a discussion. Underneath the key questions are some suggested activities the students might like to try. With very few exceptions, all the activities we've published have their equivalent online versions, and these are available as a personal curriculum in the students' online pages.

Five Leaders Tell Their Stories

Fanie Walters is a lecturer at the University of Pretoria. He and his team have been using the VESPA psychometric questionnaire to identify areas of potential support and development, allowing them to better assist undergraduates via an academic support programme. He shared the following feedback:

> **The VESPA psychometric has helped us to tailor group intervention sessions, where we can facilitate relevant activities to help develop the shortcomings identified through the questionnaires. What's most encouraging is that students have reported that the questionnaires and activities have helped them to identify and make real changes to their current approach. It has helped to move students from 'knowing' to 'doing' change.**

Fanie's clarity of vision – moving students from knowing to doing – is inspiring, and it has been gratifying to see his observations borne out in student surveys. The organisation's survey gauging student responses to the VESPA experience yielded very positive results. When asked to score the following statement from 1 (least agreement) to 5 (most agreement), 'The VESPA questionnaire and reports have helped me identify changes I need to make that I would otherwise not have identified,' the overall score was 4.45.

Thousands of miles from Fanie's South African lecture theatres and seminar rooms, *Charlotte Powell* works as a head of sixth form at Coleg Cymunedol Y Dderwen in Bridgend, between Cardiff and Swansea.

Charlotte is keenly aware of the challenges that students face as they tackle study at Key Stage 5: 'Implementing the VESPA system has helped us to support our learners to develop the skills they need to not only complete their sixth-form studies with us, but to be successful post-18 too.' Charlotte's focus is on the bespoke nature of the support that a psychometric test can support: 'The questionnaire has been crucial to enable learners to identify their areas of weakness.' She adds:

> **Not only does it match learners with bespoke tasks to help them to develop and improve their study habits, but it also generates individual coaching questions which have enabled our form tutors to provide tailored support during one-to-one mentoring sessions and identify learners that need early intervention. We would recommend the implementation of VESPA to any school's tutorial and mentoring programme.**

Neil Groves works in East Asia as head of sixth form at Bangkok International Preparatory and Secondary School in Thailand. Neil's drive and passion for his work is always in evidence when we exchange messages. 'I tried to be concise,' Neil joked when he returned his comments to us, 'but the VESPA portal is just too good.' Like Charlotte, Neil chooses to focus on the student report and its potential to strengthen the quality and depth of staff–student discussions around learning. The quality guidance his students get becomes clear: 'The reports generated inform our mentoring conversations and allow us to target those students most in need with specific questions, as well as specific VESPA activities to help build their non-cognitive skills. These conversations and activities help support their development, giving our students a better understanding of themselves.' Neil concludes, 'The VESPA portal is an invaluable resource for our pastoral team.'

Emma Lloyd is area lead for post-16 education at the Central South Consortium, overseeing professional learning and support across five of the largest local authorities in South Wales. She leads a wide-reaching, multi-school VESPA project in her region. With an energy and commitment that has been much in evidence each time we've met, Emma describes her ambition to run 'an empowering and impactful research-informed programme to support the aspirations of all learners at post-16'. 'Over twenty schools in the Central South Consortium are engaging in a professional enquiry project to develop growth mindset at post-16,' she tells us during our most recent conversation. 'The VESPA Academy platform assigns bespoke activities based on psychometric questionnaire outcomes, and generates immediate feedback to post-16 leaders and pastoral teams, providing them with all the information required for early identification of learner needs.' Emma notes how, across the schools involved, 'learners have stated they feel both supported and valued. The cycles of questionnaire support the development of impactful one-to-one coaching intervention programmes.'

'We started using the VESPA programme several years ago,' says *Phil Larter*. Phil is assistant head teacher at Queen Elizabeth's Grammar School in Faversham, Kent and shares, with Fanie, Charlotte, Neil and Emma, a deep concern with improving students' academic outcomes and life chances. 'Then,' he tells us, 'we realised that after COVID-19, our students were needing more support in developing their non-cognitive skills in order to be sure of academic success.' He adds:

> **The development of the VESPA portal has been a real game-changer because it allows us to involve a large range of students. It means we can quickly identify the intervention required with groups of students. The tutor reports with coaching questions are invaluable and the suggested activities tailored to the individual student give form time and mentoring real purpose.**

Phil finishes by pointing out that 'new developments are happening all the time, and we're excited to be able to support these and measure the impact on student development and progress'.

Phil's reference to new developments is a timely one. There have been several interesting shifts in the VESPA data over the last few years and these have prompted some bespoke adjustments or wholesale changes. Here are just two examples. Because so many students take the psychometric questionnaire each year, we can observe small changes in the nationwide attitudes expressed. Vision scores, for example, fell during the COVID-19 pandemic, and 2023 saw the first rise back up again. This led us to develop guidance for schools and colleges suggesting interventions that might help to support students who feel they're lacking direction. Another area of interest for us is retention. Early indications are that certain VESPA scores are more closely correlated with students who subsequently drop out of their studies, low vision being one of them, although it's often combined with low scores in other elements too.

It's fascinating to see these changes happening year on year, and it's rewarding to work with organisations that are seeking to support their students in ever more effective ways.

Conclusion

Ten Final Thoughts

As you might expect, we spend a lot of time researching and thinking about organisational culture.

Over the last ten years we've worked with many hundreds of schools in the UK and abroad; in the week we're writing this, schools have been in touch from Malawi and Saudi Arabia asking to use the psychometric questionnaire. We regularly have the privilege of visiting organisations as outsiders, taking the temperature of each institution, and assessing the existing culture as we walk the corridors and see communal spaces, noticeboards, canteens and classrooms, and, of course, as we meet and talk to staff.

More often than not, what we see are dedicated and hardworking teachers intent on improving themselves as practitioners, continuing professional development leads committed to improving the student experience, heads of year or key stage wrestling with challenging questions around better supporting learners, energetic lead practitioners looking to disseminate best practice – it's wonderful to observe. People like these make the places they work feel positive and hopeful, reflective and innovative.

But in the years preceding the publication of this book, our collective cultures felt the shockwaves of COVID-19. Old certainties suddenly felt fragile. The world didn't seem to work any more; things fell apart. A world like that felt hard enough as an adult. As a child, living through a period of such flux must have felt horrendous. (Where were the certainties of yesterday? What did the future hold?)

So, post-COVID-19, we need to return to our roles as patient, empathetic and positive providers of certainty. There's no room now for stories about shifting grade boundaries, rogue markers, unfair exam questions or nationwide statistical adjustments. All these messages do is suppress a student's developing sense of agency and efficacy.

Instead, we'd suggest thinking about the following.

On vision

1 High-vision students have a developing awareness of who they are, what they stand for and, therefore, what they want for their future selves. Key stages 4 and 5 are typically the times when this development accelerates and students move away from a dependency on externally imposed rewards and punishments towards an internally constructed series of values. But not everyone travels at the same speed. Activities like A Question of Money (Activity 4) or Sweet and Sour Summers (Activity 2) might be the starting point for a gradually developing vision of what interesting work might look like. Diver Goals and Thriver Goals (Activity 1) might help these ideas coalesce and these values emerge.

2 When you set a goal and attach actions to it, you put yourself on the hook. It's not always comfortable; every goal raises the spectre of potential failure. It's not surprising, in a world that seems so chaotic, that students might retreat to the safer certainties of simply hoping for the best. When we guide the setting of goals, we have to gradually decompress, beginning with short-term and low-stakes goals, and proving they can be successfully achieved rather than opening our conversations with, 'What do you want to do with your life?'

On effort

3 Often, the low-effort students we work with are working the hardest they ever have. That three hours of homework they completed last week represents a high-water mark for them. If we instruct them to 'knuckle down' or 'put in ten hours next week', it's going to be a huge challenge and seem impossible to operationalise. Effort, like a habitually exercised muscle, needs to strengthen slowly and carefully. Proactive versus Reactive (Activity 9) is a good starting point for taking small and manageable steps forward. A carefully planned Catch-Up Week (Activity 21) might be the beginning of a period in which effort levels are raised. As with

any new habit, slips can occur. When you're designing a week – or half term even – of raised effort, using Red Flag Rescue Plans (Activity 16) will help to heighten the students' awareness of the behaviours that typify a falling off of attention.

4 Sustained effort is a long game, and to begin with, its benefits compound – like anything else – relatively slowly. A student might make the decision to try really hard this term, and might manage significantly higher degrees of engagement, attention and study-directed effort for a month, only to find that no one has noticed and there doesn't seem to be any impact on their grades. It's up to us to help create a culture that rewards process as well as product. We must be aware of how students are attempting to positively transform their chances, and recognise and celebrate it when we see it happening, reassuring them that 'This will make a difference – keep going.' Never underestimate the power of catching someone doing something right.

On systems

5 There's a misconception about project management and productivity/workflow tools, and it's this: that they exist to enable us to fit even more work into our day, cramming tasks into every spare minute until we're endlessly slogging study machines. That's not what our systems activities are about. What we're trying to do is lower levels of stress, anxiety and overwhelm by increasing students' feelings of control. And, it's worth pointing out, freeing up more time for them to do the things they love. A relentless working week filled with a thousand well-organised tasks doesn't make for a happy life. In Have To, Ought To, Want To (Activity 22), we try to address this idea – that students with good systems have time to go to the cinema, meet friends, obsess about hobbies and play sports. The mark of a dedicated student is not the dropping of all these things to focus on study; it's the development of systems that allow them to exist alongside study. Balance is the aim.

6 As well as the organisation and planning of time and attention, systems refer to students' organisation of resources. In our previous books, we've extolled the virtues of task boards, and we do so again (in a fresh way, we hope!) with Pending, Doing, Done (Activity 19). As important as these systems are, the more we work with students post-COVID-19, the more we see a need to explore the initial process of note-taking, as well as the challenges of sequencing and organising those notes in a way that builds connections between ideas. Cornell Notes (Activity 23) is a good starting point here.

On practice

7 Higher utility revision strategies require greater cognitive resources. They feel harder, and because we're challenging ourselves, our fluency drops; sessions feel slow and sticky. The feelings that come with sessions like this – 'It wasn't easy' and 'I felt I was going slowly' – are understandably anxiety inducing. No wonder students return to reading and highlighting notes. But it's a false economy, and we must be on hand to explain this. However, we can't expect change to occur immediately; a one-off assembly alone won't significantly alter behaviour on its own. We should be intentional, consistent and persistent in our messaging.

8 As we saw in the Introduction, one of the things the divers and thrivers study (Beattie et al., 2016) showed about practice was the tendency of underperforming students to cram. There's a strange logic to this behaviour, and it usually goes like this: *because I use low-utility revision strategies, I tend to forget things quickly. And because I forget things quickly, there's no point in revising now. I need to do it the night before.* Once we understand this, we're better placed to correct the thinking. It's in the workshop of our long-term memories that those connections are forged and the synapses really fire. Good practice means regularly consolidating learning, connecting new learning to previous learning, doing the heavy lifting of forgetting and re-remembering old learning, and spacing practice out so that our longer term memory recasts it, connecting it with other concepts and ideas. Using Test Your Future Self (Activity 28) at the end of every topic might be a good place to start. (Students are often furious at their past selves for creating such challenging quizzes!)

On attitude

9 Low-attitude students often struggle with problem-solving because their sense of agency or control is low and levels of fatalism are high. However, we think that problem-solving is something we can demonstrate and teach. It doesn't work in the abstract, though. You need to deliver activities like 5, 5, 5 (Activity 36) and ODA (Activity 37) in response to a specific study-related issue, possibly as a coaching or one-to-one tuition session. Once the student has a problem, we're well placed to show how slower, more reflective and process-based thinking can unlock issues that initially feel impossible to solve. We suggest 5, 5, 5 as part of the whole-year curriculum in Chapter 6, but only because we've made an assumption that by week ten of term two, all students would have a study-related problem on which they could shine a spotlight. It may be that, rather than try the problem-solving activities with a whole group,

you might reserve them for your coaching curriculum.

10 We've become increasingly interested in the connection between attitude and attention. In previous books, we've looked at grit, growth mindset and buoyancy (all of which we believe have a part to play,) but post-COVID-19, we've come to appreciate the role that our attentional spotlight plays in determining how we see the world around us, as well as our place and role in it. Low-attitude students, for a range of complex and interrelated reasons, often find their attention snagged by the negative. In A Dozen Noticeboards (Activity 35), we suggest an experiment that might correct that, if only gradually.

In September 2023, the BBC reported an alarming figure. Quoting data obtained from the Student Loans Company, they outlined how university drop-out rates had risen by 28% in the five years between 2018 and 2023 (Bryson, 2023). The reasons cited in the article are various. Most telling, we think, is the analysis by the Policy Institute at King's College London and the Centre for Transforming Access and Student Outcomes in Higher Education that the primary reasons students drop out is poor mental health. These are the students who find the demands of university study overwhelming; the expectations, the deadlines, the levels of engagement and independence required. It's a decision that has significant consequences for a young person, not least financial.

But perhaps this research is also telling us something uncomfortable about the way we prepare students for the rigors of post-18 study. Tempting as it is to blame challenging contextual circumstances, maybe we need to look at ourselves too. We may well come to the conclusion that, while the students were in our care, we could have done better.

So, if we use the time we have with students to give them access to clear, replicable study tactics and behaviours, and we model them, helping learners to habitualise and embed them before university or the world of work comes along, we might be doing our learners a significant service.

Hopefully, the kind that lasts long beyond the few years through which we guide them.

References

Alhadabi, A. and Karpinski, A. C. (2020). Grit, self-efficacy, achievement orientation goals, and academic performance in university students. *International Journal of Adolescence and Youth*, 25(1), 519–535.

Bandura, A. (1982). Self-efficacy mechanism in human agency. *American Psychologist*. 37(2), 122–147.

Barton, D. (2015). What do top students do differently? *TEDxYouth@Tallinn* [video] (25 March). Available at: https://www.youtube.com/watch?v=Na8m4GPqA30.

Beattie, G., Laliberté, J-W. P. and Oreopoulos, P. (2016). Thrivers and divers: using non-academic measures to predict college success and failure. NBER Working Paper 22659. Available at: https://economics.nd.edu/assets/214055/thrivers_and_divers_using_non_academic_measures_to_predict_college_success_and_failure.pdf.

Berger, W. (2019). *The Book of Beautiful Questions* (New York: Bloomsbury).

Bjork, R. A. and Yan, V. X. (2014). The increasing importance of learning how to learn. In M. A. McDaniel, R. F. Frey, S. M. Fitzpatrick and H. L. Roediger III (eds), *Integrating Cognitive Science with Innovative Teaching in STEM Disciplines* (St Louis, MO: Washington University in St Louis Libraries), pp. 15–36.

Boyle, J. and Forchelli, G. (2014). Differences in the note-taking skills of students with high achievement, average achievement, and learning disabilities. *Learning and Individual Differences*, 35, 9–14.

Brown, M. (2023). Energy makes time. *Everything Changes* [blog] (4 August). Available at: https://everythingchanges.us/blog/energy-makes-time.

Bryson, J. (2023). University dropout rates reach new high, figures suggest. *BBC News* (28 September). Available at: https://www.bbc.co.uk/news/education-66940041.

Burnett, B. and Evans, D. (2016). *Designing Your Life: How to Build a Well-Lived, Joyful Life* (New York: Knopf Publishing).

Crum, A. J. and Langer, E. J. (2007). Mind-set matters: exercise and the placebo effect. *Psychological Science*, 18(2), 165–171.

Dagnall, N. and Denovan, A. (2017). Measuring mindset using psychometric tests. In S. Oakes and M. Griffin, *The GCSE Mindset: 40 Activities for Transforming Student Commitment, Motivation and Productivity* (Carmarthen: Crown House Publishing), pp. 211–223.

Decharnais, R., Jobin, J., Cote, C., Levesque, L. and Godin, G. (1993). Aerobic exercise and the placebo effect: a controlled study. *Psychosomatic Medicine*, 55, 149–154.

Duff, A. (2004). Understanding academic performance and progression of first-year accounting and business economics undergraduates: the role of approaches to learning and prior academic achievement. *Accounting Education*, 13(4), 409–430.

Dunlosky, J., Rawson, K., Marsh, E., Nathan, M. J. and Willingham, D. (2013). Improving students' learning with effective learning techniques: promising directions from cognitive and educational psychology. *Association for Psychological Science*, 14(1), 4–58.

Dweck, C. and Yeager, D. (2019). Mindsets: a view from two eras. *Perspectives on Psychological Science*, 14(3), 481–496.

Eyal, N. (2019). *Indistractable: How to Control Your Attention and Choose Your Life* (London: Bloomsbury).

Ferriss, T. (2015). Chris Sacca on being different and making billions (#79) [podcast] (30 May). Available at: https://tim.blog/2015/05/30/chris-sacca.

Ferriss, T. (2017). Why you should define your fears instead of your goals, *TED.com* [video] (April). Available at: https://www.ted.com/talks/tim_ferriss_why_you_should_define_your_fears_instead_of_your_goals?language=en.

Gallagher, W. (2010). *Rapt: Attention and the Focused Life* (New York: Penguin).

Greene, B., Miller, R., Crowson, H., Duke, B. and Akey, K. (2004). Predicting high school students' cognitive engagement and achievement: contributions of classroom perceptions and motivation. *Contemporary Educational Psychology*, 29(4), 462–482.

Humpherys, S. and Lazrig, I. (2021). Effects of teaching and practice of time management skills on academic performance in computer information systems courses. *Information Systems Education Journal*, 19(2), 45–51.

Jin, X. (2023). The role of effort in understanding academic achievements: empirical evidence from China. *European Journal of Psychology of Education*. https://doi.org/10.1007/s10212-023-00694-5

Job, V., Walton, G. M., Bernecker, K. and Dweck, C. S. (2015). Implicit theories about willpower predict self-regulation and grades in everyday life. *Journal of Personality and Social Psychology*, 108(4), 637–647.

Kahneman, D. and Deaton, A. (2010). High income improves evaluation of life but not emotional well-being. *Proceedings of the National Academy of Sciences*, 107(38), 16489–16493.

Kaplan, G. A. and Camacho, T. (1983). Perceived health and mortality: a nine-year follow-up of the human population laboratory cohort. *American Journal of Epidemiology*, 177(3), 292–304.

Karpicke, J. D. and Blunt, J. R. (2011). Retrieval practice produces more learning than elaborative studying with concept mapping. *Science*, 331(6018), 772–775.

Kiewra, K. A. (1985). Investigating notetaking and review: a depth of processing alternative. *Educational Psychologist*, 20, 23–32.

Kiewra, K. A., Colliot, T. and Lu, J. (2018). Note this: how to improve student notetaking. IDEA paper #73 (September). Available at: https://files.eric.ed.gov/fulltext/ED588353.pdf.

Kirk-Johnson, A., Galla, B. and Fraundorf, S. (2019). Perceiving effort as poor learning: the misinterpreted-effort hypothesis of how experienced effort and perceived learning relate to study strategy choice. *Cognitive Psychology*, 115: 101237.

Lerchenfeldt, S. and Nyland, R. (2016). Learning technique utility and preferences among second-year medical students: a pilot study of general and pre-exam study habits. Available at: https://mededpublish.org/articles/5-96.

Lewis, A. (2006). *The Seven Minute Difference: Small Steps to Big Changes* (London: Kaplan Business).

Locke, E. A. and Latham, G. P. (1990). *A Theory of Goal Setting and Task Performance* (Englewood Cliffs, NJ: Prentice-Hall). Martin, A. J. and Elliot, A. J. (2015). The role of personal best (PB) goal setting in students' academic achievement gains. *Learning and Individual Differences*, 45, 222–227.

Mark, G., Gudith, D. and Klocke, U. (2008). The cost of interrupted work: more speed and stress. Proceedings of the 2008 Conference on Human Factors in Computing Systems, Florence, Italy, 5–10 April.

Martin, A. J. and Elliot, A. J. (2015). The role of personal best (PB) goal setting in students' academic achievement gains. *Learning and Individual Differences*, 45, 222–227.

Mazza, S., Gerbier, E., Gustin, M-P., Kasikci, Z., Koenig, O., Toppino, T. C. and Magnin, M. (2016). Relearn faster and retain longer: along with practice, sleep makes perfect. *Psychological Science*, 27(10), 1321–1330.

Milkman, K. (2021). *How to Change: The Science of Getting from Where You Are to Where You Want to Be* (London: Vermilion).

Newport, C. (2005). *How to Win at College: Surprising Secrets for Success from the Country's Top Students* (New York: Crown).

Newport, C. (2010). *How To Be a High School Superstar: A Revolutionary Plan to Get Into College by Standing Out (Without Burning Out)* (New York: Broadway Books).

Newport, C. (2016). *Deep Work: Rules for Focused Success in a Distracted World* (New York: Grand Central Publishing).

Newport, C. (2022). Slow Productivity Advice, Episode 217. *The Deep Life* [podcast]. Available at: https://www.thedeeplife.com/podcasts/episodes/ep-217-slow-productivity-advice.

Oakes, S. and Griffin, M. (2016). *The A Level Mindset: 40 Activities for Transforming Student Commitment, Motivation and Productivity* (Carmarthen: Crown House Publishing).

Oakes, S. and Griffin, M. (2017). *The GCSE Mindset: 40 Activities for Transforming Student Commitment, Motivation and Productivity* (Carmarthen: Crown House Publishing).

Oakes, S. and Griffin, M. (2018). *The Student Mindset: A 30-Item Toolkit for Anyone Learning Anything* (Carmarthen: Crown House Publishing).

Ranellucci, J., Hall, N. C. and Goetz, T. (2015). Achievement goals, emotions, learning, and performance: a process model. *Motivation Science*, 1(2), 98–120.

Rau, W. and Durand, A. (2000). The academic ethic and college grades: does hard work help students to 'make the grade'? *Sociology of Education*, 73(1), 19–38.

Richardson, M., Abraham, C. and Bond, R. (2012). Psychological correlates of university students' academic performance: a systematic review and meta-analysis. *Psychology Bulletin*, 138(2), 353–387.

Stanger-Hall, K. (2012). Multiple-choice exams: an obstacle for higher-level thinking in introductory science classes. *Life Sciences Education*, 11(3), 294–306.

Stankov, L., Moroney, S. and Lee, P. Y. (2014). Confidence: the best non-cognitive predictor of academic achievement? *Educational Psychology*, 34(1), 9–28.

Świątkowski, W. and Dompnier, B. (2021). When pursuing bad goals for good reasons makes it even worse: a social value approach to performance-avoidance goal pursuit. *Social Psychology of Education*, 24(3), 653–677.

van Herpen, S. G. A., Meeuwisse, M., Hofman, W. H. A., Severiens, S. E. and Arends, L. R. (2017). Early predictors of first-year academic success at university: pre-university effort, pre-university self-efficacy, and pre-university reasons for attending university. *Educational Research and Evaluation*, 23(1–2), 52–72.

Wiseman, R. (2003). *The Luck Factor: Change Your Luck and Change Your Life* (London: Century).

Index